FAMILY MEDIATION IN EUROPE

proceedings

**4th European Conference
on Family Law**

Palais de l'Europe, Strasbourg, 1-2 October 1998

Council of Europe Publishing

French edition:

La médiation familiale en Europe

ISBN 92-871-4256-4

Council of Europe Publishing
F-67075 Strasbourg Cedex

ISBN 92-871-4257-2
© Council of Europe, April 2000
Printed in Germany

CONTENTS

Foreword..5

Programme of the Conference 7

OPENING SPEECHES

Mr Daniel TARSCHYS, Secretary General of the Council of Europe...11

Mrs Elisabeth GUIGOU, Minister of Justice, Garde des Sceaux
(France) 15

REPORTS AND SUMMARIES

1.   Introduction to family mediation in Europe and its special
      characteristics and advantages
      Report presented by Janet WALKER (United Kingdom).....................21

2.   The mediator
      Report presented by Nathalie RIOMET (France)................................39

3.   Selection, training and qualification of mediators
      Report presented by Sirpa TASKINEN (Finland) 55

4.   Relationship between family mediation and legal proceedings
      Report presented by Antonio FARINHA (Portugal)............................69

5.   The status of mediated agreements and their implementation
      Report presented by Mary LLOYD (Ireland).......................................87

6.   Promotion of and access to family mediation (Information
      programmes for access to family mediation and non-discrimination)
      Report presented by Renate WINTER (Austria) 97

GENERAL REPORT

Report presented by Igor DZIALUK (Poland)....................................113

CONCLUSIONS 121

CLOSING SPEECHES

The Right Honourable the Lord IRVINE OF LAIRG, Lord Chancellor
of Great Britain..123

Hans Christian KRÜGER, Deputy Secretary General of the Council of
Europe 129

Appendix I - List of participants 131

Appendix II - Recommendation No. R (98) 1 of the Committee of Ministers
to member States on family mediation and explanatory memorandum..........159

FOREWORD

The 4th European Conference on Family Law organised by the Council of Europe was held in the Palais de l'Europe in Strasbourg on 1 and 2 October 1998, on the topic of family mediation in Europe.

The Conference was the first follow-up action to the adoption, on 21 January 1998, of Recommendation No. R (98) 1 of the Committee of Ministers to member States on family mediation.

PROGRAME OF THE CONFERENCE

Thursday, 1 October 1998

9.30   Opening of the Conference

Welcoming words by:

. Daniel TARSCHYS, Secretary General of the Council of Europe
. Elisabeth GUIGOU, Minister of Justice, Garde des Sceaux (France)

Morning Session

Chair: Marc FISCHBACH, Judge elect at the European Court of Human Rights

10.00   **I.   Introduction to family mediation in Europe and its special characteristics and advantages**

Rapporteur: Janet WALKER, Professor, Director of the Newcastle Centre for Family Studies, University of Newcastle Upon Tyne (United Kingdom)

10.30   Discussions with panel on general questions relating to family mediation

Panel : Rapporteur + Petar ŠARČEVIĆ and Geneviève HARTLAND

11.30   **II.   Family mediation in practice: the preparation for and the process of family mediation in the context of Recommendation N° R (98) 1 on family mediation** (Demonstration and assistance by the UK College of Family Mediators)

14.30   **III.   The mediator**

- **Impartiality and neutrality**
- **Role of the mediator towards parties and with regard to the best interests of the child**

Chair: Birger HAGARD, President of the Committee on Legal Affairs and Human Rights of the Parliamentary Assembly of the Council of Europe

Rapporteur: Nathalie RIOMET, Magistrate, Director of the Private Office of the Head, responsible at interministerial level, of women's rights, Chair of the Council of Europe Committee of Experts on Family Law (CJ-FA), Paris (France)

15.00   Discussions with panel on the mediator

Panel: Rapporteur + Lisa PARKINSON and Claude LIENHARD

16.00   **IV.   Selection, training and qualification of mediators**

- **Survey of the standards and practices in force in the member States of the Council of Europe**
- **Establishment of machinery for the selection and training of mediators and to ensure that standards are achieved and maintained by mediators**

Chair: Tom COX, President of the Social, Health and Family Affairs Committee of the Parliamentary Assembly of the Council of Europe

Rapporteur: Sirpa TASKINEN, Head of Development, National Development and Research Centre for Welfare and Health (STAKES), Helsinki (Finland)

16.30   Discussions with panel on the selection, training and qualification of mediators

Panel: Rapporteur + Simon MARCOTTE and Jacques VAN DAMME

Friday, 2 October 1998

<u>Morning Session</u>

Chair: Jörg PIRRUNG, Judge at the Court of First Instance of the Court of Justice of the European Communities

9.30   **V.   Relationship between family mediation and legal proceedings**

- Establishment of the process of family mediation before, during or after legal proceedings
- The relationship mediator/judge and the powers of the judge
- Confidentiality of the discussions held during mediation

<u>Rapporteur</u>: Antonio FARINHA, State Attorney, Lecturer of Minor and Family Jurisdiction, Centre for Judiciary Studies, Lisbon (Portugal)

10.00   Discussions with panel on the relationship between family mediation and legal proceedings

<u>Panel</u>: Rapporteur + Annie BABU and Constanza MARZOTTO

11.00   **VI.   The status of mediated agreements and their implementation**

<u>Rapporteur</u>: Mary LLOYD, Service Co-ordinator, Family Mediation Service, Dublin (Ireland)

11.30   Discussions with panel on the status of mediated agreements and their implementation

<u>Panel</u>: Rapporteur + Werner SCHÜTZ and Lis RIPKE

Afternoon Session

Chair: Mary BANOTTI, Member of the European Parliament, President's Mediator for transnationally abducted children

13.30   **VII.   Transfrontier family mediation**

Discussions with Round Table on transfrontier family mediation (including Ingrid BAER and Véronique CHAUVEAU)

14.30   **VIII.   Promotion of and access to family mediation:**

- Information programmes for access to family mediation and non discrimination

Rapporteur: Renate WINTER, Judge, at present consultant at the Centre for International Crime Prevention, United Nations, Vienna (Austria)

15.00   Discussions with panel on the promotion of and access to family mediation

Panel: Rapporteur + Marianne LASSNER and Jacqueline BROWN

Final session

15h30   Proposals for further follow-up action by the Council of Europe, Margaret KILLERBY, Head of the Private Law Division, Council of Europe

15h45   Conclusions by the *General Rapporteur of the Conference*, Igor DZIALUK, Deputy Director of judicial assistance and European law, Ministry of Justice, Varsovie (Poland)

16h15   **Closing Session**

Closing words by:
. the Right Honourable the Lord IRVINE OF LAIRG, Lord Chancellor of Great Britain
. Hans Christian KRÜGER, Deputy Secretary General of the Council of Europe

Daniel TARSCHYS,
Secretary General of the Council of Europe

Minister,
Excellencies, Ladies and Gentlemen,

I am most happy to welcome all of you to the Council of Europe on the occasion of this 4th European Conference on Family Law, which is devoted to family mediation in Europe.

The Council of Europe, as you know, has a longstanding experience in matters relating to family law, as evidenced by our Conventions in this field, by a number of Recommendations, by the activities at both intergovernmental and parliamentary levels involving all the now 40 member States of the Council of Europe which is called the family of European democracy's identity.

On this occasion I particularly would like to thank Madame Elisabeth GUIGOU, Minister of Justice and "Garde des Sceaux" of France , for having accepted to open this Conference. France has had a major role in promoting family mediation and therefore it is particularly appropriate that you, Madame GUIGOU, should be with us today.

I also wish to express my thanks for the excellent reports which have been prepared by the Rapporteurs and for the many useful written contributions submitted by other participants for the benefit of this two days.

The Conference may be seen as the first follow-up action to Recommendation No. R (98) 1 on family mediation, adopted by the Ministers' Deputies in January this year. This text recommends the governments of our member States:

    - to introduce or promote family mediation
    - to take or reinforce measures necessary for that and to promote family mediation as an appropriate means of resolving family disputes.

Family mediation is one way of reducing conflict in the interest of all the members of the family, but perhaps especially in the interest of the children, who, as we are all aware, are particularly vulnerable in such situations.

Allow me to add, in this context, that two of our three previous Family Law Conferences have specifically dealt with the interests of children:

- the 1992 Conference discussed the work of ombudsmen, or similar bodies, to protect children and promote children rights
- and the 1995 Conference was concerned with family law reform regarding children.

In fact, the Council of Europe has long been concerned with the protection of children, and the level of that concern was clearly expressed in the Action Plan adopted, last October, almost exactly one year ago, by the Heads of State and Government at the Council of Europe`s Second Summit here in Strasbourg.

We have since introduced a programme for children with the aim of raising public awareness of the social challenges facing them in their everyday live. In April this year we organised a follow-up Conference to the 1996 Stockholm World Congress concerning the sexual exploitation of children, the outcome of which now forms the basis for further action in the social and legal fields of child protection and the promotion of childrens`rights and interests.

In June next year we will organise a Conference of European Ministers responsible for Family Affairs. The theme of that Conference will be "Towards a child-friendly society", a topic which has many links with the subject you are discussing at this Conference but that will obviously touch on social aspects.

Let me finally mention another Recommendation - Recommendation No. R (98)8 -, adopted by the Committee of Ministers only a few weeks ago concerning "childrens` participation in family and social life". This text calls for the appointment of an Ombudsman for children very much along the lines of your Conference to further safeguard the interests of children.

Now Recommendation No. R(98)1 which is the centre of attention here, sets out a number of principles, which will be examined during your debates today and tomorrow. These principles concern:

- the organisation of mediation
- the status of mediated agreements
- the relationship between mediation and proceedings before the judicial and other competent authorities
- the promotion of, and access to, mediation and
- the use of mediation in international matters.

Your discussions of these principles will allow for valuable and up to date information concerning the different experiences of family mediation in our different member States.

With these words I would like to wish you a successful and result-oriented debate. You can be sure that the conclusions you'll arrive at will be given further attention in the Council of Europe and I hope that they can lead to important results both here and at the national level. I now have the honour to ask Madame Elisabeth Guigou, Minister of Justice and "Garde des Sceaux" of France, to take the floor and formally open the Conference. Thank you very much.

OPENING SPEECH BY

Elisabeth GUIGOU,
Minister of Justice, Garde des Sceaux (France)

Mr Secretary General, Ladies and Gentlemen,

I am very honoured to have been invited by the Council of Europe to open the fourth European Conference on Family Law dealing with family mediation in Europe.

I should first of all like to recall Robert Schuman's pronouncement that Europe, before being a military alliance or an economic entity, should be a cultural community in the highest sense.

The Council of Europe, as we know, is founded on the essential values of personal and political freedom and rule of law.

Its activities are worthy reflections of the values of freedom and democracy which are henceforth espoused - and we all welcome this - by all European countries.

As the pioneer of the European institutions and a vital forum for Europe's democracies, the Council already has in its midst the countries of Central and Eastern Europe and has performed a considerable normative endeavour in making the law serve democracy.

Among the large number of conventions drawn up by your organisation - which were just refered to by Mr Tarschys - those relating to human rights and fundamental freedoms are basic.

While it is very active in all fields concerning human rights, the Council of Europe has also carried out very substantial work regarding legal co-operation and, specifically, family law.

In this respect, I would also emphasise the importance of the Demo-Droit and Themis programmes for legal co-operation with the countries of Central and Eastern Europe.

Inarguably, the Council of Europe can perform the role of "pathfinder" for European justice in the 21st century, as demonstrated by its three most recent lines of action for legal co-operation:

- seeking common solutions to the legal and ethical problems posed by scientific and technical progress;

- achieving more effective justice;
- modernising and harmonising national legislation.

In the family law field, international co-operation and assistance are constantly gaining strength, as witnessed by the current work relating to the preparation of an instrument on transfrontier visiting rights or the protection of legally incapacitated persons.

However, co-operation is but one facet of the importance which the Council attaches to family law.

The standard-setting achievements in this respect are numerous; I shall mention the European Convention on the recognition and execution of decisions concerning custody of children and the one on the exercise of children's rights.

You have also - here at the Council of Europe - made an institution of the staging of a European Conference on Family Law whose renown testifies to the high quality of its deliberations. Today, you have taken as the conference theme family mediation, of which the importance in the friendly settlement of family conflicts has been adknowledged by a number of European countries following its recognition in North American countries.

The importance of family mediation requires no further proof amongst those here today. But I believe that we should underline just how much family mediation helps to avoid painful separations and how it enables parents to cope, or at least to cope a little better, with the consequences of their separation, especially where their children are concerned and, assisted by the mediator, to seek a mutually acceptable solution in keeping with their situation.

The highly sensitive human dimension of family conflicts is the chief thing which makes it imperative to concentrate on seeking a solution which will appease the marital or parental dispute.

Mediation is therefore an enhancing factor in the execution of court rulings and the prevention of further litigation. It is because this solution is worked out by the actual persons concerned, or in consultation with them, that it forestalls future disputes.

Furthermore, the destructive effects of family breakdown on adults and children alike, and its more and more frequent linkage with social alienation, have been amply demonstrated in recent years. Family breakdown is often the prelude to exclusion of the poorest. Consequently family mediation also constitutes one of the means of combating social exclusion.

Family mediation is now a self-evident necessity owing to the beneficial effects which it can produce within the family unit where society is forged.

Today, saying that the family is the hub or the fundamental basis of society are well-worn expressions. But I think that this cannot be repeated enough because it is first and foremost within the family that social links are built and that the child learns the links between the generations, relations between different sexes and the relationship between freedom and authority. It is within the family that a sense of security and togetherness are to be found and for those who are fortunate enough, the family gives emotional security as the society in which we live today becomes harder and harder to deal with.

This is why family mediation should now be encouraged and developed. You are fighting, fighting for the cause of family mediation. But I believe that the authorities should do more for its development as it is a relatively new idea and like all new ideas it is still fragile.

We know that family mediation came into being in the early 1970s in the United States of America in a context where the divorce procedure forced the spouses into such uncompromising antagonism that dialogue was broken off and agreement between them was no longer possible.

The first experiments with mediation occurred in California before the process became widespread in the United States as a whole. Mediation - you know it better than anyone - subsequently developed as from 1972 in Canada where it was formalised by an Act passed in 1985 and a genuine public mediation sector was established alongside a private one.

After taking root in English-speaking countries, for example New Zealand and Australia where mediation stages are prescribed during divorce proceedings, it rapidly spread in the European countries, the United Kingdom and Belgium, with public and private mediation structures comparable to the Canadian pattern

In France, the position has been different.

Family mediation developed more tardily beginning 1988, in the absence of a procedural framework.

The takeoff of family mediation in France owes a great deal - it is even essential - to the voluntary sector. After the formation in 1988 of the "association for the advancement of family mediation", which blazed the trail, many private family mediation centres grew up.

From the outset, the public authorities, primarily the Ministry of Justice and the Ministry responsible for Social Affairs, furthered the development of these structures by granting them financial support.

Ten years on, over 120 mediation associations have links with the Ministry of Justice.

Concurrently, the field of action of these associations has changed.

17

At first they usually operated quite outside any judicial procedure although certain judicial authorities made use of family mediation on a trial-and-error basis despite the absence of a statutory and regulatory framework.

It was not until the Law of 8 February 1995 that civil mediation achieved statutory recognition, which was a very important step.

Although this 1995 legislation is not entirely specific about the role of family mediation, there can be no doubt that it was in the sphere of family conflict that this out-of-court method of resolving disputes was meant to be developed.

This method of resolving disputes out-of-court should be encouraged all the more because, to tell the truth, the increase in cases coming before the courts in all our countries has caused such a saturation of the court system that, especially regarding the sensitive question of the family, it is often difficult to spend the necessary amount of time.

This is why I presented a bill to the French parliament aiming at encouraging more alternatives to trial before a court. Family mediation should play a major role in the out-of-court methods of resolving disputes.

The French law did not set up a public mediation service, since voluntary bodies appeared in this respect to be best suited for the tasks delegated by the courts.

However, although the costs of mediation were normally to be borne by the parties to the trial, this did not prevent those with limited resources from applying for legal aid financed by public funds.

The court may, on its own initiative or at the request of the parties, designate a third party, a private individual or a legal entity, but one obviously in possession of a qualification or having the necessary training or experience in the practice of mediation, with the tasks of hearing the parties to the dispute, carefully listening to them, and weighing up their various points of view in order to seek, if possible, a solution to the conflict opposing them.

This mediation process, which is subject to the agreement of the two sides, can take effect at any point in the judicial proceedings, irrespective of whether it concerns a divorce case, a conflict of parental authority within the legitimate or natural family, or a conflict involving the right of grandparents to visit or have custody of a child.

The mediation process should be brief in order to avoid any unwarranted slowing down of the legal proceedings.

On completion of their tasks, mediators inform the court of any agreement reached between the parties, which the latter can ask the court to approve formally.

It is essential that the mediation should remain independent vis-à-vis the court throughout the mediation procedure. That is why a mediator is not required to submit a report to the court authorities.

Neither the details of the mediation process, nor the mediator's conclusions and not even the terms of the agreement reached have to be made known by the mediator.

The views exchanged during the debates in the course of these two days' proceedings will no doubt show, by reference to the situation in other Council of Europe member States, that there are different approaches to the one chosen by France for organising family mediation.

Here lies of course all the interest of this meeting. You can be assured that I will attach the greatest importance to the contents and outcome of your work.

Despite these differences, however, I am sure that all member countries are bound to share a common concern to promote this type of measure.

For my own part, I am very keen to see progress in this field and, more generally, in other methods for resolving conflicts out of court. My belief is that trying to resolve disputes before going to court simply means trying to make sure that more talking takes place, more listening takes place and that relationships are not necessarily governed by confrontation or power struggles. I am convinced that family mediation can be very beneficial to the whole of society, not only from a legal point of view but as a choice made by a society where dialogue, listening and social contact are foremost. I believe that in a society such as ours where a juxtaposition of selfish individuals is more and more common, the job done by mediators is extremely important.

This point of view seems to be widely shared by the Council of Europe.

It was at your initiative that a Recommendation on family mediation was prepared and adopted on 21 January 1998 by the Committee of Ministers.

This Recommendation establishes a number of basic principles applicable to this method of solving family disputes and provides a framework for States to apply this measure within their own domestic legislation.

Moreover, the text of the Recommendation has the added interest of mentioning the need to provide machinery for co-operation between States and encourages them to have recourse to mediation in cases of family conflicts involving foreign elements, when for example the parents are residing in different countries, have different nationalities and are fighting for custody of their children. Here mediation on a European level is a better way of resolving these conflicts that we just don't know how to deal with today.

The organisational difficulties entailed in granting the right of transfrontier visits and custody, the improper removal of children to another country, with all the attendant suffering for the parents and the child (let us imagine their childhood memories) show that, in this respect, international family mediation might be an appropriate process for settling parental differences. States try as much as possible to make this work, taking into account the differences in laws, the differences, all too frequent, in the decisions of national courts and also taking into account the personal situation of parents who are unable to find a common ground of discussion. This is the reason why States should reflect on the notion of international family mediation and the value of appointing persons of high calibre and great moral authority when the State's own action and the respect for judicial decisions has reached a dead end.

This and the many other aspects of this question bear witness to the many advantages of this institution.

The Recommendation adopted by your Organisation and the proceedings of this Conference, which promise to be very fruitful in view of the diversity of the chosen themes and the quality of the speakers, will, I have no doubt, encourage those States which do not yet practice this system to introduce it.

The earlier European Conference on Family Law, held in Cadiz in 1995, was devoted to the theme of the future of family law.

In our own day and age when families are undergoing such profound changes, when models are diversifying and family ties are tending to weaken, instruments for defusing tensions such as family mediation are more than ever essential and there can be no doubt that they will be incorporated in the family law of tomorrow.

INTRODUCTION TO FAMILY MEDIATION IN EUROPE AND ITS SPECIAL CHARACTERISTICS AND ADVANTAGES

Report presented by

Janet WALKER
Professor
Director of the Relate Centre for Family Studies
University of Newcastle upon Tyne
United Kingdom

Summary

Recommendation No. R 98(1) is an important landmark in the field of Family Law in Europe since it encourages Member States to introduce, promote and strengthen family mediation as an appropriate process for the resolution of family disputes, particularly those which involve children and arise during marital separation and divorce.

Family disputes involve emotional and personal relationships; they impact on other family members, notably children; and the parties in dispute may be required to maintain continuing and constructive relationships as parents. While legal processes may undermine these fragile relationships, family mediation is designed to promote communication and reduce conflict. Parties are facilitated to negotiate their own agreed joint decisions with the help of an impartial mediator who has no authority to impose a settlement. Family mediation is a distinctive process which parties usually enter voluntarily and within which discussions are confidential.

It is a relatively new process in Europe, although some States have been developing family mediation over several decades and have incorporated it into their judicial and administrative procedures. Mediation may be organised in a number of ways, although the process is broadly similar, with mediators subscribing to a set of common principles and recognising the importance of training, and the maintenance of quality standards. As co-operation across States increases, there is likely to be a growing demand for mediation in family matters which crosses national boundaries. Family mediation upholds the importance of family life to children and the need for social support for parents who separate and divorce. Research has shown that mediation is not appropriate for all families, but for those who do mediate successfully, the quality of life can be much improved.

This is an exciting time for Family Law in Europe. There are opportunities for States to embrace mediation thereby paying special attention to the interests of children who will be given the best chance of recovering from the experience of divorce if they maintain good relationships with both parents and live in an environment which is not ravaged by conflict.

Family Mediation in Europe

Family Mediation In Context

Ten years ago in Lisbon the European Ministers of Justice examined the question of the interests of the child. They recommended that the Committee of Ministers of the Council of Europe should instruct the European Committee on Legal Cooperation to pay special attention to a number of matters including the use of 'the friendly settlement procedure' to protect the best interests of the child. At that time this process of 'friendly settlement' was commonly referred to as 'conciliation' in those States where it existed. In recent years, however, the term 'conciliation' has largely been replaced by the term 'family mediation'. It denotes a method of resolving disputes which is usually established as an alternative to legal procedures through the courts – alternative dispute resolution. The area of family law with which it has become most closely associated is that of marital separation and divorce, a matter which has been considered carefully at the Council of Europe for a long time.

This meeting in Strasbourg is the Fourth European Conference on Family Law to be held under the auspices of the Council of Europe. One of the four topics debated at the first Conference in Vienna in 1977 related to the grounds for and consequences of divorce. The second conference, held in Budapest in 1992, addressed, amongst other things, the issue of parental separation and remarriage within the context of parental responsibilities; the legal provisions to prevent and reduce disputes in divorce cases; and alternative methods of solving family disputes. The last conference, held in Cadiz in 1995, dealt with family law in the future, and family mediation was on the agenda. Following that meeting, the Committee of Experts on Family Law set up a Working Group to consider mediation and other processes to resolve family disputes. Recommendation No. R (98)1 on family mediation was adopted by the Committee of Ministers in January this year.

It is an important landmark in the field of family law in Europe since it recommends that member States should introduce or promote family mediation where it does not currently exist, and strengthen it wherever necessary in those States where mediation has already been introduced. Quite clearly, the Recommendation embraces and endorses conciliatory approaches to the resolution of disputes which arise in family relationships, most notably during marriage breakdown. Why is this Recommendation important?

The rapid pace of social change in most western countries in the last twenty years has been characterised by falling marriage rates and rising divorce rates. New trends in marital behaviour show that a growing number of young people postpone marriage, or do not marry at all. Legal marriage, once considered to be the only legitimate form of partnership has given way to cohabitation arrangements. Although the incidence of divorce varies between countries, there is not a single country in Europe which has not experienced an increase in the numbers of marriages ending in divorce.[1] (Until recently, of course, divorce in Ireland was not allowed, but marriages still broke down). According to a study undertaken in Vienna in 1977, based on divorce trends at that time it was predicted that about 85 per cent of marriages in Europe would be dissolved by the year 2000.[2]

Not surprisingly, many States have sought to reform their family laws in the last 20 years. There is widespread agreement that the family is at the heart of society, and that it provides the best environment for the raising of children. Therefore, the breakdown of family relationships can never be an intrinsically good thing, but of course, the primary concern is the potentially detrimental impact of parental separation and divorce on children. The most recent review of over 200 studies on divorce and the outcomes for children[3] has found that children of separated families have a higher probability of living in poverty and poor housing; being poorer as adults; behavioural problems; performing less well in school; needing medical treatment; leaving school and home at an early age; becoming sexually active, pregnant, or a parent at a young age; depressive symptoms, high levels of smoking and drinking, and drug use during adolescence and adulthood. These outcomes are affected by financial hardship; family conflict before, during and after separation; multiple changes in family structure; loss of contact with the non-resident or non-custodial parent; and the parents' ability to recover from the distress of divorce. The policy implications are clear:

- parents need support to deal with the distress of separation and divorce to enable them to give better help to their children

- parents need information so that they can understand how their marital separation and particularly conflict, can be detrimental to their children

- legal processes and support services need to facilitate the continuing involvement of non-custodial/non-residential parents in their children's lives (except where protection from abuse and violence is necessary)

- parents and children need help and support at times of transition, for example when step-families are being formed

We can conclude that stable post-divorce arrangements and the maintenance of good relationships with their mother, father and wider kin give children the best chance of recovering from the experience of divorce.[4]

By contrast, when parental relationships are conflictual, children may find themselves caught in the middle between two painfully divided households where ongoing hostility and bitterness are commonplace.[5] These children are likely to be the ones who suffer the most, especially if they lose contact with one of their parents. In reality it is often the non-residential father who gives up when communication has broken down completely, and maintaining parental responsibility has become an impossible struggle.[6] Given this evidence, it is clear that when couples enter the legal process of

24

separation and divorce, a heavy responsibility is placed on those seeking to settle disputes which can so easily arise in the intense emotional contexts which exist during this highly personal transition. To ignore the special characteristics of family disputes or to perceive them as no different to any others in civil law is to seriously jeopardise and undermine the needs and best interests of children. Indeed, it has been argued that using lawyers and the courts to settle matrimonial disputes is the least constructive way, since traditional legal processes are not well suited to the resolution of sensitive family issues.

Unlike any other area of dispute to which mediation has been applied, discussion about the resolution of matrimonial disputes requires governments to address an issue which is imbued with personal, moral and religious values. While disputes within industry, commerce and the community are regarded as an almost inevitable fact of life, those which arise within families, and particularly those which emerge during the process of divorce, are viewed as an indication of 'failure' in interpersonal relationships which it ought to be possible to avoid. Even the language used – marriage *breakdown* – symbolises the sense of disaster and disappointment surrounding the dissolution of the marriage contract. Thus, dispute resolution mechanisms are frequently expected to address the underlying social issues as well as settle the emergent disputes.

Family disputes usually involve emotional and personal relationships in which feelings can exacerbate the difficulties, or disguise the true nature of the conflicts and disagreements. Furthermore, disputes which arise during the process of separation and divorce impact on other family members, notably children who may not be included in any dispute resolution process, but whose interests may be considered paramount. In such cases, the parties in dispute are expected to have continuing and interdependent relationships as parents, and the dispute resolution process needs to facilitate constructive relationships for the future in addition to enabling the resolution of current disputes.[7] It is widely recognised amongst professionals and researchers that marriage breakdown is rarely easy, and almost always painful and distressing. However well managed, divorce normally results in intense feelings of grief, sadness, rejection, anger, bitterness, hostility and an overwhelming sense of loss. It has been described as the second most stressful life event for adults after the death of a spouse.[8] As personal and social networks disintegrate and financial pressures bite, resentment increases, communication is further strained, and conflict flourishes.[9] These are just the kinds of conditions which undermine parenting abilities and cause the greatest difficulties for children.

A growing body of research demonstrates that marital separation and divorce is a *process* which usually begins years before the legal divorce, and has repercussions which reverberate for a long time afterwards.[10] The legal process of dissolution of a marriage should, therefore, take these factors into account. It has been suggested[11] that interventions in matrimonial disputes should be 'person-oriented' rather than 'act-oriented', suggesting that mediation is far better suited than formal mechanisms to the sensitive issues surrounding family disputes.

Understanding Mediation

Mediation is a process in which an impartial third party, the mediator, assists parties to a dispute to negotiate their own agreed joint decisions. The mediator has no power of coercion, does not act as a judge or adjudicator, arbitrator, or advocate for either of the parties. The mediator has no authority to impose a settlement on the parties, and discussions are normally confidential. Mediation, then, offers an alternative to negotiation by lawyers and to adjudication by the courts or administrative authorities.

Family mediation is a distinctive and discrete process. Of course, families spend much of their time resolving disputes which arise in the normal course of events in daily living, and most have some competencies in the practice of 'private ordering'. During the trials and tribulations of marriage breakdown, however, conflict resolution skills are in high demand, and while some couples maintain a problem-solving approach, others find it difficult to do so unaided. While the law is a blunt instrument with which to deal with personal problems, mediation, on the other hand, appears to offer a much more appropriate level of support, and is relatively cost effective judged against four criteria for evaluating methods of conflict resolution: their ability to settle the dispute; the cost of the process; the justice of both process and outcome; and the promotion of social goals.[12]

The relative merits of alternative processes of dispute resolution, and in particular, family mediation, have been variously embraced and challenged in many jurisdictions since the mid 1970s. The potential benefits of an approach which encourages the parties to sit down together and talk with the help of an impartial, skilled mediator have been widely acknowledged. In addition, family mediation has been shown to reduce conflict and improve communication between the parties thus increasing the quality of life for family members experiencing separation and divorce.[13] Mediation has been described as 'the gradual creation of order and co-ordination between the parties'[14] and if all the issues can be settled in mediation it seems that the benefits survive the test of time.

In contemporary discussions about family mediation it is easy to overlook the fact that most of the communities in Africa, Asia, Latin America, China and Japan have developed informal mechanisms for settling disputes through mediation. In addition, extended family and kinship circles have provided a mediation resource in many cultures.[15] Japan, with its long cultural tradition of mediation, emphasises the importance of restoring harmony, and of mutual apology and pardon.[16] Zehr[17] has talked about the 'restorative lens' in bringing the reintegrative emphasis into focus. The creation of harmony between disputants who share or have shared an intimate relationship, or who have continuing responsibilities together (as parents, for example) would seem to be an eminently sensible goal of any dispute resolution process. True resolution must involve some level of mutual acceptance, forgiveness and a desire for cooperation.[18] Gehm[19] has emphasised the need to 'let go' of conflict and to 'make amends' for past hurts. All these would appear to be extremely important if the best interests of children are to be protected when their parents separate.

The process of mediation aims to do more than simply promote settlements although this must be the ultimate goal. Family mediation aims

- to help parties to reach workable settlements which are in the best interests of the children involved and which take account of the needs of adults

- to reduce the extent and level of conflict between the parties, and improve communication

- to promote shared parental responsibility for the future care of children

Mediation focuses on the present and the future, but it cannot ignore the past. A process of consensual decision-making can help parties to come to terms with the ending of their relationship, although mediation is not counselling or therapy. Nor does mediation set out to help parties to be reconciled and to save their marriage, although some couples do decide to attempt reconciliation as a result of facing the stark realities of a life apart during the mediation process.

Family Mediation in Europe

The use of family mediation as an alternative to judicial or administrative decision-making is a relatively new process in Europe although mediation has been used for a long time in traditional societies for the resolution of disputes within communities and kinship systems, and more recently in western societies for the resolution of commercial and industrial disputes. In Europe, as in North America, developments in family mediation have been ad-hoc, with no international legal instrument to establish the basic principles and main directions of family mediation. The initiative has frequently been left to enthusiastic professionals, including lawyers, psychologists and social workers to develop mediation services either annexed to the courts, or based within the community, independently of the legal process.

In 1997, the Working Party on Mediation and other Processes to Resolve Family Disputes invited States represented on the European Committee on Legal Cooperation to provide information about the use of family mediation in family matters. Completed questionnaires were received from twelve States, from which it was clear that the aims and objectives of a mediation process were largely similar, although different States use differing terminology to describe mediation. Furthermore, despite the uncoordinated way in which family mediation has developed and the inevitable existence of a wide variety of practice styles and settings, most family mediators appear to share a common set of principles:

- mediation is conducted in private and discussions are confidential

- the parties retain responsibility for formulating their own agreements based on their own needs and circumstances, with an emphasis not on rights and wrongs but on establishing a workable solution

27

- mediators are impartial, and remain neutral as to outcomes, although they take responsibility for encouraging direct communication, and full and frank disclosure between the parties, balancing power and reducing the level of conflict

- mediation focuses on future relationships and arrangements, believing that parents know what is best for their children.

Based on these principles, the mediation process in most States seeks to enhance communication, maximise the exploration of alternatives, address the needs of all parties, help parties to reach agreements perceived by them as fair, and provide a model for future conflict resolution.[20]

Research has shown that putting pressure on parties to mediate against their will is not effective, and may actually increase the hostility and further escalate conflict.[21] On the other hand, making it compulsory for parties to meet either separately or together to explore the relevance of and suitability for mediation is increasingly accepted as a sensible way of introducing parties to the potential benefits of a process which may be ill-understood and about which there may be unnecessary fears. The new Family Law Act 1996 in England and Wales, for example, adopts this approach, making it compulsory for a partner who wishes to apply for state funding (legal aid) for legal representation, to attend before a family mediator to assess whether or not they are suitable for mediation before the application for state funding can be considered. The intention is to reduce the number of couples who negotiate at arms' length and to encourage a more conciliatory process. The only country in Europe in which attendance at mediation is compulsory is Norway. In Norway, spouses who have children under 16 have to attend mediation before their separation and divorce can be brought to a court or county Governor. Although research in Norway indicates that parents do not object to this requirement, in fact mediation is not necessary or relevant in all cases, rendering it a potentially costly provision. In the majority of States, mediation is considered to be a process which parties enter voluntarily, and the right of each party to seek independent legal advice is upheld. Mediators are not expected to give legal advice.

As family mediation gains a more prominent and more secure position as an alternative dispute resolution process, and as policymakers accept the need to find better ways of resolving family disputes, there is increasing demand for a more standard framework for the establishment and regulation of mediation. Recommendation No. R 98(1) does just that. It aims to assist and provide member States of the Council of Europe with a framework for the development of family mediation.

The Scope of Family Mediation

In principle, there need be no limit on the scope of family mediation, and the Recommendation gives States latitude to include family situations as defined in their respective legislation. In reality, however, because the concern for children whose parents separate has been the main influence on the development of family mediation, most family mediators focus on the

28

resolution of disputes about arrangements for children, most commonly issues to do with custody or residence, and with access to or contact with the non-custodial parent, or to other family members. In most countries, the pioneers of family mediation traditionally came from professions where the focus was on protecting children's interests. Usually, mediators have been psychologists, social workers and lawyers, and many have worked within the setting of the court, sometimes responsible for making assessments about arrangements for children.

Increasingly, however, it is becoming clear that it is not always possible to separate custody and access disputes from those relating to finance and property matters. Although a division between child-related and finance-related disputes appeared to make sense for the professionals concerned, it became apparent that it was not necessarily in the best interests of the couples using mediation. While couples were being encouraged to be civilised and cooperative in settling matters to do with children, they frequently had to use court processes to settle disputes about all the other issues. The absurdity of couples talking together about their children one day, and arguing about financial matters in court through their respective lawyers on another was starkly revealed in our major study of mediation in England and Wales[22] carried out in the late 1980s. Couples who could not agree about arrangements for children were equally likely to be in dispute about other matters. At the end of our study as many as 25 per cent of couples who had successfully mediated child issues were still in dispute about child maintenance payments, and some 27 per cent about property matters. Furthermore, the lastingness of settlements mediated in isolation from other disputes was problematic. Hence we recommended that not only should mediation be all-embracing, capable of dealing with all the issues consequent on separation and divorce, but also that it could not be considered as a true alternative dispute resolution mechanism while parties are obliged to settle other disputes through other processes. By the late 1980s mediators in England had begun to realise the limitations of a narrow child-focused approach, and began to develop training which would give them the knowledge and skills to deal with all the issues which couples have to negotiate when they divorce. Offering parties the opportunity to settle all disputes within mediation is an attractive alternative to using lawyers and the courts, and is now increasingly standard practice in North America and some European countries.

Although most States focus in mediation on children's interests, and on the importance of both parents maintaining contact and good relationships with their children, it is usually possible to include other matters. In Poland and Slovenia, for example, financial and property disputes are specifically included in the discussions about the scope of mediation. The inclusion of other issues has led in some countries, particularly in England and Wales, to an increasing number of lawyers training as mediators. Sometimes they mediate with a psychologist or social worker so providing a complementary combination of skills.

Recent research in England has compared the short and longer-term effectiveness of mediation on all issues compared to mediation in respect of

29

child-only issues.[23] Some three to four years after mediation, people who attempted to settle all issues in mediation were more likely to feel that mediation helped them maintain good relationships with their ex-spouse and to feel less bitter; to feel more content with child-care arrangements and to have experienced fewer disagreements about access and contact; and to believe that mediation had enabled them to reach agreements which could stand the test of time. One of the most significant findings from this research is that actually reaching agreements in mediation is an important factor in respect of accruing longer-term benefits which have a substantial impact on the quality of post-divorce life.

The Organisation of Mediation

Family mediation has developed in different ways in different jurisdictions and there are no universally preferred organisational arrangements. When States have taken responsibility for organising or promoting mediation services, they are often attached to courts or to administrative authorities. In other countries, although the State or municipal authorities have taken a considerable amount of responsibility for the organisation of mediation, the service is not attached to the courts, but may be provided through other authorised Ministries or agencies. Where mediation has been developed independently of State authorities, it is primarily provided by professionals within counselling, social welfare or youth services, working in local communities although they may be coordinated by a national body. In some countries, mediation is provided in statutory and independent services with no one clear model being preferred.

State-organised services are normally provided free or through legal aid provisions. Increasingly, mediation is offered privately and fees are charged. Unlike jurisdictions in North America, however, there are relatively few private mediators in Europe charging a fee for service, and where they do practice, the number of people using their services tends to be small. France and England are almost certainly the two countries where there is the most private activity, although in some other States charges are made for mediation provided by public or voluntary bodies.

Research demonstrates that the practice setting makes a difference in terms of both process and outcome.[24] Setting seems to act as a significant constraint, shaping what mediators do or do not do. Mediation attached to courts or administrative authorities sometimes restricts the time available, limiting opportunity for a more therapeutic process spread over several months. Stress on settlement-seeking in such settings puts pressure on mediators and parties alike, with reaching agreements taking precedence over attempts at reducing conflict and improving communication between the parties. Bargaining in the very obvious 'shadow of the law'[25] might promote speedier settlements, but the process is one which seems to provide rather less satisfaction for the parties than one which is not operating to a judicial or administrative timetable.

Whatever the organisational arrangements, mediation should be available to all without discrimination, and quality standards need to be maintained irrespective of the fact that mediation practice is varied. It has been suggested that family mediators should be fully cognisant of the psychodynamics of marriage breakdown, its emotional fluctuations and accompanying anguish; they should be knowledgeable in behavioural dynamics and family systems; and they should have a thorough knowledge of family law as it affects the parties. Procedures for the selection, training and accreditation of mediators are likely to vary in different countries. Although most mediators have been drawn from the professions of law, psychology and social work, a high degree of flexibility in relation to previous qualifications and experience would appear to be constructive.

The Process of Mediation

Mediation has been described as 'an intricate modern dance that includes legal, economic and emotional themes'.[26] As in all dances, mediators have identified steps, variations on which are constantly being perfected. Whatever theoretical or professional orientation the mediator identifies with, the mediation process usually comprises a set of steps or stages each of which has goals, tasks and attendant mediator skills. Most mediators adhere to a more or less structured approach to the mediation process, although this needs to be balanced with a degree of flexibility to accommodate the unique characteristics and experiences of each family.

Mediation involves redefining and interpreting a problem or situation in such a way that renders mutual problem-solving and negotiation more feasible. This is not easy for the mediator or for the parties. Traditionally, superior bargaining power is seen as a strength – each party weighs up their relative strengths in order to win. Balancing power towards a win-win outcome creates a considerable tension.[27] The mediation process gives each party the opportunity to explore whether they have something to gain from reaching agreement and less to lose than they might have imagined. The mediator should not take sides in this process but should prevent manipulative, threatening or intimidating behaviour by either party. Unlike a lawyer, who acts for one of the parties and represents his or her own point of view, the mediator is not acting for either party, and as such has no authority to give advice. However, mediators can and do give information about legal issues, or indicate what factors might be taken into account when a judicial or administrative decision is taken about issues in dispute. There is a fine distinction between giving information which is appropriate within mediation, and giving advice which is not. Mediators often suggest that parties should seek independent legal advice before, during, or following mediation.

Some researchers[28] have suggested that mediators may subtly shape agreements particularly in respect of arrangements for children, but ideally, mediators should remain neutral, recognising that parents almost certainly know best what is in the interests of their children. Statements made during the course of mediation which indicate that a child has suffered or is at risk of suffering serious harm or abuse however, are unlikely to be viewed as confidential by the mediator who will encourage parents to seek appropriate help, or may be obliged to disclose such information to the appropriate authorities.

31

Feminist critics of mediation have expressed concerns that unless the imbalance of power between parties is addressed, women in particular may be bullied during face-to-face negotiations into agreeing unfair settlements by domineering or even abusive husbands.[29] As a result, most mediators ensure that mechanisms exist to ascertain the safety of the parties and any history of domestic violence or abuse between them. If one party is in fear of the other, it may be more appropriate to terminate the mediation process, although the fact that violence has been a feature of the relationship in the past should not automatically preclude the possibility that mediation may be appropriate. Adequate attention to and screening for domestic violence are now well accepted pre-requisites in assessing whether both parties are willing and able to negotiate effectively.

Mediation is considered to be a relatively brief intervention, not requiring more than a few sessions over a relatively short period of time. The greater the conflict, and the more issues there are in dispute the longer the process might take to reach completion. In North America it has been perfectly acceptable for mediators to employ therapeutic approaches, which may well increase the amount of time spent in mediation. In Europe, by contrast, there are more examples of a more legalistic, problem-solving approach being used. Most mediators find it helpful to have a framework which views the family as an interacting system.[30] They also appreciate the central role that communication plays in any process of dispute management. Communicative behaviour, verbal and non-verbal creates, reflects and remediates conflicts.[31] Resolving conflicts means finding solutions through effective communication that meets the needs of all the parties concerned. But mediation does not take place in a vacuum: there are contextual issues which shape interventions and outcomes. While traditional methods of dispute resolution pay particular attention to outcomes, often insensitive to the relationships between the parties, alternative mechanisms have seen as critical the interpersonal conflicts inherent in disputes in the private domain of the family. Three features of a communication approach applicable to family mediation have been identified[32]: the examination of micro-elements of behaviour with emphasis on patterning; a focus on dynamic, developmental features of negotiation; and an effort to uncover how meaning is dependent on relational, social and cultural contexts. A communication perspective has emerged as well-suited to the practice of family mediation, not least because of its emphasis on process.

Mediators are well aware that the best negotiated agreements may still falter when put into practice. Time is often given to the couple to try arrangements out and then to review them. Each may wish to take legal advice about the settlements to ensure that they are not seriously prejudicial to one person's best interests. In England, the majority of those mediating their disputes seek independent legal advice before and/or after the mediation process. Since it is not usual for advising lawyers to attend the mediation sessions, mediators always encourage their clients to discuss settlements with their lawyers if they have them. Our research indicates that this acts as a safeguard against either party making agreements which could have unforeseen adverse consequences, and is much appreciated by the users of mediation. In practice, few agreements get unpicked by lawyers at this stage.

Mediation is probably unique among conflict resolution processes because it can create a process for future review and revision regardless of whether there are any problems or concerns. The time taken for mediation is dependent on the number of issues in dispute, their complexity, the extent and severity of conflict between the parties, each party's willingness to compromise, and any barriers to negotiation which the mediator may need to address. Research has shown that unless parties are enabled to acknowledge and to some extent deal with contentious pasts, then they are less able to work together on building co-operative futures.[33] Mediators do need to be aware, however, that some people may wish to dwell on the past in order to delay the divorce process, and this cannot be acceptable. Mediators must be skillful directors of a complex and demanding process, capable of remaining detached enough to function as impartial professionals, yet sensitive to the position of each party.

The Status of Mediated Agreements

In most countries, the agreements reached in mediation are recorded in some kind of document and copies given to the parties. In Germany and Norway, these agreements are considered to be legally binding, although this is not the norm elsewhere, but even so, they are not usually enforceable unless and until they have been endorsed by the appropriate judicial or administrative authority.

Some people who mediate are profoundly disappointed that at the end of an intensive period of negotiation the agreements reached do not carry the same weight or authority as court-imposed solutions. Increasingly, mediators are assisting parties to draw up their agreements into a relevant 'legal' document which can be reviewed, if necessary, by each party's legal advisor. As mediators become increasingly competent then there is growing judicial respect for the agreements reached and greater acceptance within the legal profession of mediation as a viable method of alternative dispute resolution. The fact that mediation is conducted in private, and that discussions are considered to be confidential, should not undermine the status of agreements reached.

Looking to the Future

Recommendation No. R(98)1 of the Committee of Ministers is a major step forward in the recognition of alternative dispute resolution and family mediation in family law. It does not in any way undermine every citizen's right of access to the law, nor diminish the powers of judicial or administrative authorities to protect the interests of all family members caught up in the misery of marital disputes. Family mediation upholds the importance of family life to children and the need for broad social support for both parents as they each have common responsibilities for the upbringing of children. It also recognises that children are people with human rights, and that they need to be informed of or allowed to participate in family proceedings which affect them. Mediators take responsibility for reminding parents of the need to inform and consult their children about changes in their lives, and in some

States, mediators either include children in part of the mediation process, or provide supportive counselling services for children.

It is known that many parents find it difficult to comply with decisions which are imposed by judicial or administrative authorities, whereas decisions reached consensually during a process which is designed to empower them to retain responsibility for their respective futures and those of their children, have a better chance of standing the test of time. But mediation is not an easy option, nor is it possible for everyone to benefit from it. During its formative years, great claims were made for mediation as a superior way for parties to resolve disputes and those claims went largely unchallenged. The attraction of mediation is in many ways related to its apparent simplicity as a process which encourages men and women to just sit down and talk. Yet it is far from being a simple process. It is important not to be so enthusiastic about family mediation that its limitations are overlooked. For some people the bitterness is too deep, the disputes are too entrenched, and the personal costs associated with negotiating face-to-face are estimated to be too high. Forcing people into mediation is not likely to be a cost-effective approach, and States are urged to be realistic about the extent to which mediation can become the norm. There is now a respectable body of research which can guide policy and practice. Early studies of mediation concentrated on measuring settlement rates which vary between 50 and 80 per cent, but this is rather limited given that the focus in mediation is on process as well as outcomes. Research shows[34] that mediation does assist in the recreation of friendly relationships, and that parties are helped to cope with stress, reduce resentment and tension, and improve communication between them. There is also some, albeit limited, evidence that mediation can substantially reduce the economic as well as the social cost of divorce.

There is no consensus among the available studies as to the best predictors of achieving mediated agreements, although mediators favouring a problem-solving approach seem to be more effective than those who are more settlement-oriented. The parties also seem to prefer the former, too. There is some evidence[35] that agreement is more likely if parties perceive that the mediator can help them to gain insight into their feelings; when disputes are relatively recent and less severe; and when parties possess good communication skills and are willing to cooperate. It seems that what people value most about family mediation is its ability to enable them to take their own decisions and work out their own arrangements. What the process is called (cooperation talks; friendly settlements; or mediation) and how it is defined and organised is far less important than what it does, whether it meets the varying needs of divorcing couples, and whether mediators are professionally competent.

As mediation develops across Europe, there are demands for increased professionalism and for both national and international standards. Quality assurance is increasingly central to the challenges facing States. Many bodies are developing national standards for mediator selection, training and accreditation. This is particularly important if mediation is to be applied to the increasing number of family disputes in which there is an international element. Cases of international abduction can be extremely damaging for all concerned, especially the children, and lead to protracted legal proceedings in more than one jurisdiction. With growing cooperation across States there is much to be done to minimise conflict between parents and encourage them to reach consensual agreements at an early stage in custody and access disputes thereby preventing the improper removal or retention of a child in as many cases as possible. Disputes which arise between parents living in different States are often the most difficult to manage because of the involvement of more than one judicial authority, and the potential for parents to live far apart. Mediation should be considered as an appropriate option even when the parties are resident in different States. International mediators will need additional training, and to be sensitive to different cultural influences and expectations. They will also need to work flexibly in order to mediate across geographical as well as judicial boundaries. Nevertheless, all the principles of mediation must apply. As populations become increasingly mobile there is considerable potential for mediation to vastly improve the lives of children who travel between States in order to benefit from a continuing relationship with both parents.

This is an exciting and challenging time for family law in Europe. It is not helpful to be overly prescriptive about how mediation should work, but more constructive to offer choice and a variety of approaches. There is clearly a limit to the extent to which any State should or could control the process, although it should facilitate its development and availability. Mediation should be an autonomous process which can take place before, during or after legal proceedings.

In many countries the take up of family mediation remains low. To some extent this reflects the lack of good information about its unique characteristics and potential benefits, and more attention may need to be paid to its promotion. In reality, it is to be expected that some people will decide that mediation is not for them, or that it is too difficult or upsetting. Divorce is painful for most people, and although mediation may seem to be a very sensible option, no-one should underestimate the considerable courage choosing to mediate disputes may take, nor the challenge of rebuilding trust between the parties. However well it works, family mediation is not a panacea nor can it take away all the bitterness. Some couples can manage it, others cannot. There is both a public and a private interest in the making and remaking of cooperative relationships, and all States have an interest in the furtherance of civility within family life. The Recommendation encourages States to develop and promote dispute resolution processes which best fit their particular needs while bearing in mind the principles of family mediation which render it unique.

As we approach the millennium the predictions are that current trends in marriage and divorce will continue, and that we will see many types of family and varying living arrangements. Nevertheless, concern for the interest of children, and the belief in family life as the building block of society are unlikely to diminish. Family mediation is likely to play an important role in the way in which States respond to these issues.

[1] Boh, K. *'Family Life Patterns – A Reappraisal* in K Boh', M Bak C Clason M Pankratova, J Qvortrup, GB Sgritta and K Waerness, (eds) *Changing Patterns of European Family Life* (1989) London Routledge.

[2] Wiegman, B. Das Ende der Hausfraueneche, Plädoyer gegen eine trügerische Existenz grundlage, (1980) Hamburg.

[3] Rodgers, B., and Pryor, J., *Divorce and separation: the outcomes for children.* York, Joseph Rowntree Foundation (1998).

[4] Morrison, D.R. and Cherlin, A.J. (1992) The Divorce Process and Young Children's Well-being: A Prospective Analysis', *Journal of Marriage and the Family,* vol. 57, pp. 800-12.

[5] Cummings, EM and Davies, P. *Children and Marital Conflict: The Impact of Family Dispute and Resolution* (1994) New York. The Guilford Press.

[6] Simpson, B, McCarthy, P and Walker, J. *Being There: Fathers After Divorce,* (1995) Newcastle upon Tyne: Relate Centre for Family Studies, Newcastle University.

[7] Sander, F.E.A. 'Towards a Functional Analysis of Family Process', in J. Eekelaar, and S.N. Katz (eds), *The Resolution of Family Conflict: Comparative Legal Perspectives.* (1984). Toronto: Butterworths.

[8] Holmes, T.H. and Rahe, R.H. (1967) 'Homes-Rahe Social Adjustment Rating Scale', *Journal of Psychosomatic Research,* vol 11.

[9] McCarthy, P., Simpson, B., Walker, J. and Corlyon J. (1991) Longitudinal Study of the Impact of Different Dispute Resolution Process on Post-divorce Relationships between Parents and Children.Report to the Fund for Research on Dispute Resolution (Newcastle upon Tyne: Family and Community Dispute Research Centre, Newcastle University).

[10] Kiernan, K.E. (1991) 'What About the Children?', *Family Policy Bulletin,* December (London: Family Policy Studies Centre).

[11] Fuller, L. (1971) 'Mediation - Its Forms and Functions', *Southern California Law Review,* 44, pp. 301-28

[12] MacDougall, D.J. (1984) 'Negotiated Settlement of Family Disputes', in J. Eekelaar and S.N. Katz (eds) *The Resolution of Family Conflict: Comparative Legal Perspectives* (Toronto: Butterworths).

[13] Walker, J., McCarthy, P. and Timms, N. (1994) *Mediation: The Making and Remaking of Cooperative Relationships* (Newcastle upon Tyne: Relate Centre for Family Studies, Newcastle University).

[14] Gulliver, P.H. *Disputes and Negotiations: A Cross-Cultural Perspective* (1979) London. Academic Press.

[15] Vroom, P., Fassett, D. and Wakefield, R.A. (1981) 'Mediation: The Wave of the Future?'. *American Family,* 4, pp. 8-13.

[16]Schimazu, I. (1984) 'Procedural Aspects of Marriage Dissolution in Japan', in J.M. Eekelaar and S.N. Katz (eds) *The Resolution of Family Conflict: Comparative Legal Perspectives* (Toronto: Butterworths). Wasgatsuma, H. and Rossett, A. (1986) 'The Implications of Apology: Law and Culture in Japan and the United States', *Law and Society Review,* 20, pp. 461-498.

[17] Zehr, H. (1990) *Changing Lenses* (Scottsdale, Pennsylvania: Herald Press).

[18] Walker, J. (1992) 'Mediation in Divorce: Does the Process Match the Rhetoric?', in H. Messmer and H-U Otto (eds) *Restorative Justice on Trial* (Dordrecht: Kluwer Academic Publications).

[19] Gehm, J.R. (1992) 'The Function of Forgiveness in the Criminal Justice System', in H. Messmer and H-U Otto (eds) *Restorative Justice on Trial* (Dordrecht: Kluwer Academic Publications).

[20] Walker, J. 'Family Mediation' in J Macfarlane, (ed) *Rethinking Disputes: The Mediation Alternative* (1997) London: Cavendish Publishing Ltd.

[21] Conciliation Project Unit, *Report on the Costs and Effectiveness of Conciliation in England and Wales,*(1989) London: Lord Chancellor's Department.

[22] Conciliation Project Unit, *Report on the Costs and Effectiveness of Conciliation in England and Wales,* (1989) London: Lord Chancellor's Department.

[23] McCarthy, P, and Walker, J. *Evaluating the Longer Term Impact of Family Mediation* (1996), Newcastle upon Tyne: Relate Centre for Family Studies, Newcastle University.

[24] Irving, HH and Benjamin, M. *Family Mediation: Contemporary Issues* (1995), Thousand Oaks, California, Sage.

[25] Mnookin, RH, and Kornhauser, L. 'Bargaining in the Shadow of the Law: The Case for Divorce' (1979), *Yale Law Journal 88 p.950.*

[26] Kaslow, F. (1988) 'The Psychological Dimension of Divorce Mediation', in J. Folberg and A. Milne (eds) *Divorce Mediation: Theory and Practice* (New York: The Guildford Press).

[27] Mnookin, RH. 'Why Negotiations Fail' *Ohio State Journal on Dispute Resolution* (1993) Vol 8:2 at 238-249.

[28] Dingwall, R, and Greatbatch, D. 'Behind Closed Doors: A Preliminary Report on Mediator/Client Interaction in England' (1991) *Family and Conciliation Courts Review* Vol.29 at 291-303.

[29] Grillo, T. 'The Mediation Alternative: Process Dangers for Women' (1991) *Yale Law Journal* 100(6) at 1545-1610. Hart, BJ. 'Gentle Jeopardy: The Further Endangerment of Battered Women and Children in Custody Mediation' (1990) *Mediation Quarterly* 9(4) at 317-30. San Francisco. Jossey-Bass.

[30] Gee, I. and Elliott, D., (1990 'Conciliation - A Family Model', in T. Fisher (ed) *Family Conciliation within the UK: Policy and Practice* (Bristol: Family Law).

[31] Folger, J.P., Poole, M.S. and Stutman, R. (1993) *Working Through Conflict: Strategies for Relationships, Groups and Organisations* (New York: Harper Collins).Hocker, J.L. and Wilmott, W.W. (1992) *Interpersonal Conflict,* 3rd edition (Dubique, IA: William C. Brown).Folger, J.P. and Jones, T.S. (eds) (1994) *New Directions in Mediation: Communication, Research and Perspectives* (Thousand Oaks, Calif: Sage).

[32] Putnam, L.L. and Roloff, M. (1992) 'Communication Perspectives on Negotiation', in L.L. Putnam and M. Roloff (eds) *Communication and Negotiation* (Newbury Park, Calif: Sage).

[33] McCarthy, P, Simpson, R, Walker, J and Corlyon, J. *Longitudinal Study of the Impact of Different Dispute Resolution Process on Post-divorce Relationships between Parents and Children. Report to the Fund of Research on Dispute Resolution* (1991), Newcastle upon Tyne: Family and Community Dispute Research Centre, Newcastle University.

[34] Walker, J. Update on UK Research, in *UK College of Family Mediators Directory and Handbook* (1998), London. Sweet & Maxwell.

[35] Pearson, J and Thoennes, N. 'A Preliminary Portrait of Client Reactions to Three Court Mediation Programs' (1985) *Conciliation Courts Review* 23(1) at 1-14.

THE MEDIATOR

Report presented by

Nathalie RIOMET,
Magistrate, Director of the Private Office of the Head,
Responsible at interministerial level of women's rights,
Chair of the Council of Europe Committee of experts
on Family Mediation (CJ-FA),
Paris, France

Summary

The principles set out in the Recommendation are based mainly on the notions of impartiality and neutrality.

Family mediation, as a way of settling conflicts amicably, is a relatively recent innovation in most member States. However, the process is undeniably governed by a certain number of precise rules, which can be laid down and qualified in domestic legislation.

Impartiality applies to mediators themselves and to the triangular relationship that is a specific feature of mediation. The absence of any leaning towards one or other party enables the protagonists to arrive at a negotiated settlement of the dispute which divides them, with the help of a third party.

While the neutrality requirement is associated more with the process itself, that is the outcome of the conflict, it increases the parties' autonomy and creates a favourable climate for lasting agreements which respect the interests of each member of the family, in particular the children.

Mediators are therefore the guarantors of a set of ethical principles specifically applicable to mediation, in which impartiality and neutrality have an identical role.

Over and above this complementarity, the ethics of mediation give rise to other guiding principles, enshrined in the European Convention on the Exercise of Children's Rights, which are essential for restoring equality within the couple and taking the children's well-being and best interests into account.

*

*   *

Report

THE MEDIATOR

Impartiality and neutrality
Role of the mediator towards parties
and with regard to the best interests of the child

It is mediators themselves who are the focus of this afternoon's proceedings. We will consider mediators from the standpoint of the qualities required for the proper conduct of the mediation process and the types of training of this third party, in the broadest sense, that this implies.

More specifically, mediators will be looked at from two perspectives: their impartiality and neutrality, which as we shall see are essential if mediation is to be conducted successfully, and their role in relation to the parties and with regard to the best interests of the child.

Mediation is by definition a triangular process, characterised by the intervention in a dispute of a third party, generally deemed to be impartial and neutral.

The recommendation stresses these two aspects in its preamble and the principles it lays down and makes them requirements for mediators in their relationship with parties and children in negotiations to secure common agreements.

Neutrality and impartiality are particularly necessary in the specific context of mediation in family disputes for two reasons.

The first concerns the affective implications of family disputes and the second the fact that the protagonists in any conflict are not the only persons concerned by the outcome of the separation. A couple's children are every bit as much affected, at least as far as future changes to their life style are concerned, yet are unable to take a direct part in solving the conflict.

The relatively recent introduction of mediation into national legislation invites a comparison of how the concepts of impartiality and neutrality are applied in each of the alternative methods of conflict resolution offered by contemporary society: the intervention of the courts and/or that of a mediator. (I)

An examination of the specific nature of the mediation process and of family conflict from the standpoint of the interests of those concerned, including not only the parents but also the couple's children, highlights other major principles governing the way the process is conducted. (II)

40

I.   The mediator as guarantor of certain ethical principles

Mediation is traditionally seen in terms of the ethical principles of impartiality and neutrality.

Any consideration of these principles needs to focus on two aspects:

- firstly, the relationship between these two required qualities of mediators, and

- secondly, other principles likely to contribute to the success of mediation in the specific context of family disputes.

The application of these concepts to neighbouring fields, particularly the judicial process, offers a number of interesting bases for comparison which can help to clarify the notions of impartiality and neutrality in the mediation process.

A.   *Impartiality and neutrality as hierarchical concepts in the judicial process*

All the mediator's obligations in a triangular relationship stem from impartiality while neutrality is associated with the functional aspect of the process and its goal: conflict resolution and/or drawing up an agreement.

There is thus a dual focus: the mediator, with the main feature of his or her involvement being the ability not to take sides, which means restoring equality between the parties, and the process itself, which is supposed to foster the autonomy of the parties to disputes with a view to achieving a lasting settlement.

1.   *Impartiality: a traditional concept*

Impartiality is a quality associated with mediators and can be defined negatively as the absence of any positive or negative preconceptions regarding either of the parties. This quality has particular significance in a triangular relationship. Mediation obviously gives the first example of this type of relationship. However, impartiality first became an established principle in the judicial setting.

Modern constitutions do not make impartiality a specific obligation of judges.   The main foundation for the judiciary is its independence. Independence and impartiality are therefore interdependent, with the former serving as the basis for the latter, though it is not expressly referred to.

The notion of impartiality is given content in national legislation in provisions concerning incompatibility, the right to challenge judges and reasonable suspicion of bias, coupled with the existence of judicial supervisory and disciplinary bodies such as the French *Conseil supérieur de la magistrature* (the country's judicial services commission).

In practice though, it is article 6.1 of the European Convention on Human Rights that has come to enshrine judicial impartiality as a fundamental right of litigants.

For example, in the Piersack v Belgium judgment of 1 October 1982, in which the Court was required to rule on the successive exercise of different responsibilities during the same set of proceedings, it found that in order to decide whether a court was impartial within the meaning of article 6.1 of the European Convention on Human Rights, it had to take into account not only the personal conviction of a given judge in a given case, that is a subjective approach, but also whether he offered sufficient guarantees to exclude any legitimate doubt in this respect, an objective approach.

Schematically the Court therefore assesses the suspicions and fears which a party to proceedings might harbour towards a judge and examines the factors likely to alter the judge's impartiality from the standpoint of the apparent conduct and progress of the proceedings.

The Court's case-law gives a particular light on the procedural rules in force in national legislation. Various principles enshrine the need in all circumstances for judges to distance themselves from the parties, such as the objective examination of all the facts for consideration, respect for the principle that all parties should be heard at all stages of the proceedings, consideration of all the parties' claims and ensuring that the grounds for a decision are justified by the facts of the case.

Although judicial ethics are always closely bound up with the concept of impartiality, this is not the case with neutrality.

2.   *Neutrality: an overshadowed concept*

Neutrality must also be seen in negative terms, but this time in the context of the need to achieve a result. It can thus be described as the absence of a personal position on any particular situation.

In the judicial field it has a residual role since the judge's function is, in essence, to reach decisions in disputes by applying the relevant rules of law and deciding between competing claims.

Admittedly, the power of conciliation forms part of judges' functions but reconciling the parties' points of view in order to reach a mutually acceptable settlement seems to be secondary to their main task of hearing cases and ruling on conflicts, albeit while seeking a fair outcome.

Given the way the role of judges and the nature of certain types of dispute have evolved, flexibility is required to reach solutions with which all parties can agree, in particular with the help of the range of possibilities available when cases are being prepared. There are several parameters to the search for a legal outcome consistent with the facts placed before the courts but in order to prepare the reasoning on which a court's decision is based it is not necessary for judges to be neutral.

42

When judges do not succeed in reconciling the parties, they must make a ruling, in accordance with the terms of the application. In civil proceedings, it should be remembered, it is the parties who, through their claims, determine the pattern of the proceedings, in which they answer each other by means of written submissions and, where appropriate, cross-claims, with the result that the courts must settle points submitted to them and may not grant more or less than has been claimed (neither "*infra*" nor "*ultra petita*").

It has to be acknowledged that judges' powers of reconciliation cannot be made mandatory and are constrained by the adversarial nature of proceedings.

Neutrality therefore has to be seen in the context of the dispute as the parties themselves define it while decision making is part of the very nature of the judicial function.

In other words, the concept of neutrality is not a direct part of the judicial process. It simply means that any decision must only reflect the proceedings and respond to the parties' claims, with the judge having no personal interest.

Finally, there appears to be no possibility of complementarity or hierarchy between the two concepts, with only impartiality having the status of a fundamental principle.

The situation regarding mediation, judicial or otherwise, is quite different, which is what distinguishes this procedure from other forms of intervention in conflicts and ensures its autonomy vis-à-vis the judicial institution.

B. Impartiality and neutrality: two complementary concepts in mediation

The relationship between these two concepts enables us to identify a certain number of criteria, which constitute both the outlines of a definition and a practical approach.

In the context of family mediation, impartiality and neutrality are generally described as being complementary, and even indistinguishable. However, they are usually perceived in hierarchical terms, with impartiality the higher ranked and in some ways encompassing neutrality.

In practice, it would be more correct to present these notions as guiding principles that are incorporated into rules that are best suited to meeting the challenges thrown up by conflicts: restoring communication and protecting the children.

Mediators do not guarantee an agreement but a method. This notion, borrowed from the sociologist Jacques Faget, forms the basis for the obligations placed on mediators, which serve as guarantees to the parties to conflicts.

1. The principles laid down in the Recommendation

The Council of Europe Recommendation is both a compromise document and an educational tool of considerable scope. Various principles are laid down to help establish and encourage mediation, based on the rules found in the national legislation of member States where family mediation has been institutionalised and the experiments being conducted in various countries.

Impartiality and neutrality are of equal importance in drawing up guiding principles, designed to encourage, in the broadest sense, the resolution of family conflicts and protect the well-being and the best interests of the children concerned.

Several provisions relate to the application of the principle of impartiality. Part III of the principles, concerned with the mediation process, provides certain clarifications to the statement that "the mediator is impartial between the parties". Item iii states that "the mediator respects the point of view of the parties and preserves the equality of their bargaining positions".

Equality between the parties is fundamental and is both a feature of and a specific obligation in family mediation. Bargaining, in the sense of the search for mutual agreement, cannot succeed in the absence of equality and may thus give rise to agreements that will not be respected, or even a series of judicial disputes.

The issue of marital violence has to be seen in the light of the need for equality: item ix usefully makes the point that in the event of violence, it first has to be decided whether mediation is appropriate, given that such violence is in itself a source of inequality between the parties.

Therefore mediators must quickly establish a diagnosis on the context of the separation. In this respect, they must also prevent in the course of the process any possible risk. The organisation of separate meetings with each of the parties – called causus – might prove necessary in order to stop any violences, provided that this activity of the mediator, which is not specifically connected to the question of violences, be clearly explained to the parties.

Both mediators themselves and the mediation process must help to restore a climate of confidence and belief in the proposed instrument for resolving the conflict.

The nature of the separating couple's social environment can be very important. Such a separation is often accompanied by a break with their circle of friends or even the surrounding family. In such circumstances, the influence of third parties is generally in direct proportion to the difficulties the parties themselves have in finding a solution. It follows that the intervention of a third party who is external to the conflict must not reproduce the ambivalence that the parties encounter in their immediate environment.

This places a number of obligations on mediators:

- not taking either parent's side is at the heart of the mediation process;

- the parties must have the same opportunity to express their views, state their positions and so on;

- mediators must not substitute for those professionally qualified to offer legal advice;

- they must respect parties' private lives; item v of Part II is the logical consequence of impartiality: respect for private lives and the absence of any personal considerations on the mediator's part are essential safeguards for the parties. This principle also applies to the confidentiality of discussions, particularly in cases where the parties might decide to take their cases to, or back to, the courts.

Turning to neutrality, reference is often made to the parties' reappropriating the conflict and re-establishing their autonomy as a measure of family mediation's effectiveness. As stated in the preamble to the Council of Europe Recommendation, "family disputes involve persons who, by definition, will have interdependent and continued relationships".

It is this criterion which probably underlies the autonomy of family mediation and its superiority over other methods of settling disputes amicably.

Item ii illustrates the purpose of neutrality, which is to achieve an outcome to the process with, where appropriate, an agreement. Paragraph 7 of the preamble also casts light on this notion.

"The parents are the negotiators, the mediator is a third party who facilitates discussion, guides the process and is responsible for it, but not for the outcome". Haynes' 1989 definition gives rise to two fundamental notions: the self-determination of the parties and the mediator's non-interference in the solution to the conflict.

Conducting the process neutrally therefore implies a number of standards:

- mediators must listen to the parties, be able to reformulate the different aspects of the discussion and ensure that the issues at stake are fully understood. These skills may be summarised by the notion of non-directed discussions;

- mediators must focus on the interests at stake rather than simply on positions. The key to this is the ability to differentiate personality issues from the matters at dispute;

- mediators must enable parties themselves to make proposals, since it is they who have to make the choices.

45

2. *The necessary link between these two guiding principles*

The process will not fulfil its purpose in the absence of impartiality and neutrality. Failure to observe either creates problems. The two concepts are therefore equally important in family mediation.

Neutrality is probably the most delicate of these skills. There are two pitfalls to be avoided: that on the basis of their past experience mediators seek to impose on the parties solutions that seem from the outset to meet the problems, or that they are excessively ambitious in carrying out their functions.

The same problem arises when, in order to be made legally binding, the agreement reached between the parties has to be approved by the courts.

The scope of these two principles is not confined simply to their own content. A whole body of other rules and principles flow from them, varying from country to country. When viewed as standards they form the basis of a detailed code of ethics of family mediation.

Protecting the best interests of the children and of the parties to the conflict raises a specific issue which is proper to family mediation.

II. **The mediator's role with regard to the parties' interests and the best interests of the child**

It seems logical in fact to reverse the above order and consider the mediator's role firstly in terms of the children's interests.

The Recommendation originated in the work of the Committee of Experts on Family Law, and more specifically the Convention on the Exercise of Children's Rights.

Article 13 of the Convention is the first reference in an international instrument to the possibility of using family mediation. However, the work that led to the drafting of the Recommendation was imbued with the entire philosophy of the Convention.

Under it, children must be considered to be persons recognised by law in their own right and enjoying rights, particularly procedural ones, as full family members.

From this standpoint, the success of family mediation must be seen in terms of a positive outcome of the separation for the children, made possible by the mediator's ability to make the parents aware of the new organisation of the family, the relations between each of its members and the needs of each one.

46

A.   *The children's best interests*

As far as their role vis-à-vis children is concerned, mediators must be guided above all by item viii of Part III of the Recommendation.

The notion of children's best interests is difficult to define, given the range of parameters involved. According to Dean Carbonnier, since a child's interest takes many forms, it can be viewed from the outside in many ways so that in the end the notion becomes too vague to provide an objective principle that can be applied.

Turning more specifically to children whose parents are separating, the sociologist Irène Théry says the debate can only make sense when seen in the context of a complex system of social regulation of the family environment.

To take the matter further, the child's interests may be seen as both a criterion and an objective, whose common factor is time.

Whatever their age, children whose parents separate are often forced to adapt suddenly to their new circumstances and must completely redefine their environment and life style. Several studies have shown that children in this situation pass through various stages and experience strong feelings of sadness, aggression, guilt and instability.

This means that discussions relating to the consequences of a separation for the children cannot be confined to deciding where they will live but must also be concerned with them as individuals and with their basic needs, desires and, more broadly, feelings, both now and in the future.

The Convention on the Exercise of Children's Rights is in this sense: informing them of family proceedings that concern them and giving them the opportunity to express their feelings and opinions and thus to participate directly or indirectly in the mediation process.

How do mediators safeguard children's best interests?

The issues at stake are the following:

- help parents to look beyond their dispute as a couple to discuss the children and exchange ideas on the children's current and future needs. It can be difficult for parents to be objective spokespersons for their children because they are very often polarised by their own conflict and suffering. It is therefore the mediator's task to persuade the parents to talk about how they perceive their children's needs. Mediators must also make sure that outside the mediation framework, parents communicate with their children on a sound basis;
- enable parents to make the practical arrangements for relations between themselves and their children, particularly regarding periods spent with each of them. Mediation encourages collaboration and communication rather than competition between parents, thus giving

them a feeling of responsibility for decisions concerning their children, after properly assessing their needs. The reference point must therefore be the children's interests, rather than giving priority to the parents's interests.

Views vary as to whether it is appropriate for children to be present during the mediation process.

Some believe that the children's presence at several sessions can help indirectly to make parents more aware of their joint responsibilities. At the very least, it gives the children the opportunity to express their views, thus avoiding the feeling they often have of being pushed on one side.

Others consider that involving children in the actual proceedings may be too delicate a matter. They stress the need to shelter children from their parents' conflict. In these circumstances, it may be thought preferable to try other approaches, such as bringing together children whose parents are involved in mediation, to enable them to express their views.

In every case, children need to be informed about the separation, with the explanations, adjusted to take account of their age, preferably being supplied by both parents.

Mediators also act as ramparts against decisions that would not be in children's best interests.

The Recommendation calls on member States to provide for urgent measures to be taken if necessary.

However, the fact that such provision is made in domestic legislation must not prevent mediators from remaining extremely vigilant.

Indeed, family mediators carry a specific responsibility in cases where they fail to divulge information they receive about ill-treatment.

## B.	*The parties to the conflict*

The legal and social spheres look at the issue of the intervention of third parties in the case of couples in difficulty solely from the standpoint of the mandate granted by an authority.

As has been seen, family mediators' role vis-à-vis the parties is multifaceted. Impartiality and neutrality require them to operate a strict code of practice. Yet over and above the relevant rules laid down in each country's legislation, several issues emerge concerned with the general policy which each country has to lay down.

Mediators' independence of the parties and the courts offers an initial illustration of the options for organising family mediation.

Jean Bonafé-Schmitt distinguishes three types of legitimacy relating to how mediators are appointed:

Delegated legitimacy derives from legislation or a judicial authority: in this case, the court hearing a dispute appoints a mediator in the course of the proceedings.

Professional legitimacy derives from mediators' professional skills.

Finally, social legitimacy indicates that a mediator has been chosen by the parties with no external reference.

When legitimacy is defined in terms of the method of appointment, it can be analysed with reference to the two extremes of the proposed classification.

The way family mediation is organised, if appropriate, in the form of a public service, makes it necessary to offer certain safeguards to those to whom mediation is proposed.

The voluntary chararacter which is given to this measure by certain legislations supports this consideration.

In contrast, in the absence of any state machinery the parties are totally free to choose their own mediator but are also less well protected with regard to his or her qualifications. It would therefore be appropriate for Member States to provide, one way or another, some form of supervisory machinery.

In every case, the parties must be free to decide whether or not to undergo mediation and, where appropriate, return to the court to which their dispute was originally referred to terminate the process.

The Recommendation touches on another issue. This concerns the relationship between mediation and other forms of qualified intervention in disputes. Just how far does a mediator's role with respect to the parties extend? The Recommendation excludes them from giving legal advice, which is traditionally the domain of clearly identified professionals such as lawyers.

Mediators and lawyers thus appear to have complementary roles, each being required to confine themselves to their specific terms of reference towards parties.

The same applies to other professionals, such as notaries or psychologists, whom the parties might wish to introduce into the process or whom mediators might refer to as part of a multidisciplinary approach. In such cases the mediator acts as the "conductor", with the authority to guide the parties, in accordance with their interests and the complexity of one or other aspects of the dispute, towards the relevant resource person.

CONCLUSION

Mediators all have their own particular background - difficulties for them to detach themselves from particular views of couples, families and affective relationships are not negligible -.

The ability to overcome the questions and, to a certain extent, what might be described as personal problematics, requires substantive work and great maturity.

Managing conflicts, with the different forms they take and the range of special problems experienced by each member of the family, calls for real qualifications, know-how and appropriate experience.

These are the challenges posed by an autonomous process of conflict resolution which will develop, in particular with the support of effective machinery for training and selecting mediators.

REFERENCES

Richard Abel (Ed.), **The Politics of Informal Justice**, New York, Academic Press, 1982.

Annales de Vaucresson, "les paradoxes de la médiation", n° 2/1988.

Association pour la promotion de la médiation familiale, "Charte européenne de la formation des médiateurs exerçant dans les situations de divorce et de séparation", (APMF, Espace XV, 14 rue des Frères Moranes, 75015 Paris).

J. Auerbach, **Justice without Law? Resolving disputes without lawyers,** New York, Oxford University Press, 1983

Annie Babu, Maryvonne David-Jougnaud, Stéphane Ditchev, Alain Girot, Pierette Aufière, Isabella Biletta, Noëlle Mariller, **Médiation familiale, regards croisés et perspectives,** Erès, 1997

Benoît Bastard, Laura Cardia-Vonèche, **Le divorce autrement: la médiation familiale**, Paris, Syros, 1990.

Benoît Bastard, Laura Cardia-Vonèche, "L'irrésistible difusion de la médiation familiale", **Annales de Vaucresson**, n° 29, 1998/2, pp. 169-198.

Benoît Bastard, Laura Cardia-Vonèche, "La médiation", **Information sociales,** n° 28, 1993, pp. 84-93.

Nicolas Blain, John Goodman, Joseph Loewenberg, "La médiation, la conciliation et l'arbitrage. Comparaison internationale entre l'Australie, la Grande-Bretagne et les Etats-Unis", **Revue internationale du travail**, Vol. 126, N° 2, mars-avril 1987, pp. 199-220.

Jean-Pierre Bonafé-Smitt, **La médiation, une justice douce,** Syros.

Laura Cardia-Vonèche, Benoît Bastard, "Vers un nouvel ordre familial?", **Le groupe familial**, n° 125, 1989, pp. 123-129.

Jocelyne Dahan, **La médiation familiale,** Essentialis, 1996.

Gwynn David, Simon Roberts, **Access to Agreement,** London, Open University Press Book, 1998.

Robert Dingwall, John Eckelaar (Eds), **Divorce Mediation and the Legal Process,** Oxford, Clarendon press, 1988.

Joseph Duss-von Werdt, Gisela Mähler, Hans-Georg Mähler (Eds.), **Mediation: Die andere Scheidung, Ein Interdsiziplinärer Uberblick, Stuttgart,** Klett-Cota, 1995.

Jacques Faget, **La médiation,** Erès, 1997.

David Greatbatch, Robert Dingwall, **Selective Facilitation: Some Preliminary Observations on a Strategy Used by Divorce Mediatior,** Oxford, Centre for Socio-Legal Studies, 1989, 35 p., dact.

Trina Grillo, "The Mediation Alternative: Process Danger for Women", **Yale Law Journal,** n° 100, 1991, p. 1545 et suivantes.

John M. Haynes, **Divorce Mediation, A practical Guide for Therapists and Counselors**, New York, Springer, 1981.

Institut suisse de droit comparé et Faculté de droit de l'Université de Genève (CETEL). La médiation: un mode alternatif de résolution des conflits, Schulthess Polygraphister Verlag, Zürich, 1992, pp. 263-265.

Howard H. Irving, Michael Benjamin, **Family Mediation, Theory and Practice of Dispute Resolution**, Toronto, Carswell, 1987.

Lisette Lauren-Boyer et alii., **La médiation familiale**, Paris, Bayard, Coll. Travail social, 1993.

Muriel Laroque, Marie Théault, **Notre enfant d'abord: le divorce et la médiation familiale,** Paris, Albin Michel, 1994.

Etienne Le Roy, "Les pratiques de médiation et le droit: spécificité de la problématique française contemporaine", Annales de Vaucresson, n° 29, 1988/2, pp. 63-76.

Mediation Quarterly (Revue de *The Academy of Family Mediators,* Jossey-Bass Publishers, USA).

Claude Martin, **Les médiations familiales: structures modèles d'intervention, publics et rapports au judiciaire. Justice pour tous ou justice communautariste?** Rapport pour le service de la recherche du ministère de la Justice, Avril 1994.

Jessica Pearson, Nancy Thoeness, "Divorce Mediation: An Overview of Research Results", **Columbia Journal of Law and Social Problems,** Vol. 19, N° 4, 1985, pp. 451-484.

Simon Roberts, "Three Models of Family Mediation", in R. Dingwall et J. Eekelaar (Eds.), **Divorce mediation and the Legal Process,** Oxford, Clarendon Press, 1988, pp. 144-149.

Jean-François Six, **Le temps des médiateurs,** Paris, Seuil, 198?.

Jean-François Six, **Dynamiques de la médiation,** 1997.

Lucienne Topor, **La médiation familiale,** Paris, Puf. Coll. Que sais-je?, 1992.

Lois Vanderkooi, Jessica Pearson, "Mediation Divorce Disputes: Mediator Behaviors, Styles and Roles", **Family Relations**, 1983, N° 32, pp. 557-566.

Bailly (Y), Bazier (F), Boubault (G), Filiozat (I) (sous la direction de) **"La médiation"**, Non violence Actualité, Montargis, 1993, 88 p.

Duriez (P) **"Les médiations en France: vers un état des lieux - tome I - Les écrits - 1980-1994"**, CLCJ, 1994, 81 p.

Fisher (R), Ury (W) **"Comment réussir une négociation"**, Seuil, 1982.

Guillaume-Hofnung (M) **"La médiation"** PUF, Que Sais-je? n° 2930, 128 p.

Perrin (J-F), Widmer (P) (sous la direction de) **"La médiation: un mode alternatif de résolution des conflits"**, Publications de l'Institut suisse de droit comparé, 19, Genève, 1992, 384 p.

Touzard (H) **"La médiation et la résolution des conflits"**, PUF, Paris, 1977, 420 p.

Babu (A), Bastard (B) (tous la direction de) **"La médiation dans tous ses états"** Le Groupe Familial n° 125/1989, 138 p.

"Actes du colloque organisé par le CRPC sur la médiation" Archives de Politique Criminelle, n° 14/1992, 182 p.

"Médiation interculturelle: actes de la formation 1992-1993", EN FAS Renue de l'Education Nationale-Fonds d'Action Sociale, n° 5, 130 p.

CLCJ (Comité de Liaison des Associations Socio-Educatives de Contrôle Judiciaire) **"La médiation"** Le Bulletin, n° 8/1986, 126 p.

"Négociation et médiation dans l'entreprise", Communication et Organisation, 1997, 369 p.

SELECTION, TRAINING AND QUALIFICATION OF MEDIATORS

Report presented by

Sirpa TASKINEN
Head of Development
National Development and Research Centre
for Welfare and Health (Stakes),
Helsinki, Finland

Summary

Since divorce mediation is a relatively new phenomenon in Europe, only a few countries have established permanent training systems for mediators. In different countries the role and function of mediation vary considerably, and thus also the qualification, selection and training of the mediators and the applied methods in mediation differ from each other.

People who need training in mediation can be divided into three categories. First there are professionals who may encounter underlying marital stress in the course of their jobs, though it may not be possible or appropriate for them to work directly with it. They must know enough to be able to recognise it, take account of it and perhaps make well-timed and sensitive referrals. Second are those such as social workers and family doctors who have a wide range of duties and who, in the course of these, either choose or find themselves obliged to undertake some marital work. And third there is a relatively new group of professionals in agencies, which specialise in mediation.

Although the following working methods can be overlapping, or even used in succession, there seem to be at least four different kinds (or stages) of mediation in Europe:

1.   Mediation (more specifically, reconciliation) aiming for re-uniting of the spouses

2.   Mediation   (more specifically, conciliation) as a means to reach agreements upon matters arising from the breakdown

3.   Mediation as a conflict solving method in marital conflicts, breakdown and divorce

4.   Mediation supporting deeper understanding and personal growth of family members.

These different aims call for different training. The training programs vary from one week up to two years. A new era is beginning in 1998, as the Institut universitaire Kurt Bösch (Sion, Valais) will arrange a post-graduate training qualification in mediation. There are several partner universities collaborating in the program. A course called "European Master in Mediation" will be arranged from November 1998 to December 2000. Candidates for the European Masters in Mediation will normally:

- hold a university first degree giving access to postgraduate study;

- have had initial mediation training and three years' experience in conflict management, but alternative qualifications will also be considered.

There are several stages of training, which should be available in all countries: short basic introductory courses, advanced courses, and possibility to specialise in mediation. However, on this phase of development, it is easy to agree with the recommendations of the Committee of Ministers to Member States on Family Mediation that it would be premature to implement more formal requirements in this area until mediation is more widely practised at a European level.

Report

1.   Need for training

Since divorce mediation is a relatively new phenomenon in Europe, only a few countries have established permanent training systems for mediators. In different countries the role and function of mediation vary considerably, and thus also the qualification, selection and training of the mediators and the applied methods in mediation differ from each other.

People who need training in mediation can be divided into three categories.[1] First there are professionals who may encounter underlying marital stress in the course of their jobs, though it may not be possible or appropriate for them to work directly with it. They must know enough to be able to recognise it, take account of it and perhaps make well-timed and sensitive referrals.   Second are those such as social workers and family doctors who have a wide range of duties and who, in the course of these, either choose or find themselves obliged to undertake some marital work. And third there is a relatively new group of professionals in agencies, which specialise in mediation.

In relation to these categories, there are three stages of training; basic, in-service and advanced. During basic training, a student needs to acquire sufficient understanding of the dynamics of marriage and family interaction to understand their implications for her/his future work and to recognise the opportunities for intervention or referral appropriate to her/his agency and when her/his own knowledge and skill are not enough. S/he needs to acquire enough confidence to start applying her/his knowledge while recognising that training is a continuous process. This first stage of training in one form or other is necessary for those in all three categories of work.

The second, in-service, level of training also applies to all three categories of work. The specialist and generalist workers will need some in-service training focused especially on referral and on coping with cases which they cannot refer.

The third and more advanced level of training is appropriate for specialised mediators as well as those whose more general duties involve mediation, and especially if they have to teach and supervise others.

2.   Forms of mediation

In this paper, the term 'mediation' is used in a broad sense, since the variation in the working methods and objectives seems to be wide. Thus the term 'mediation' can be used as a synonym to 'marriage counselling'; in this paper it also covers 'reconciliation' (i.e. the attempt to re-unite the spouses) and 'conciliation' (i.e. assisting the partners to deal with the consequences of the established breakdown of their marriage). In some countries, family mediation means problem solving in marital and family disagreements in general, and further, assisting partners to gain deeper understanding in their mutual relationship and the family situation. Nowadays it is not usually expected that mediation would eliminate marital breakdown if the partners have made up their mind. Instead, it is expected to give the couple a chance to reflect their marriage with an objective expert, to get information on marital matters and divorce, and to make the necessary agreements.

Thus, although the following working methods can be overlapping, or even used in succession, there seem to be at least four different kinds (or stages) of mediation in Europe:

1.   Mediation (more specifically, reconciliation) aiming for re-uniting of the spouses

2.   Mediation (more specifically, conciliation) as a means to reach agreements upon matters arising from the breakdown

3.   Mediation as a conflict solving method in marital conflicts, breakdown and divorce

4.   Mediation supporting deeper understanding and personal growth of family members

Accordingly, these different objectives lead to different training programs and qualifications for the mediators. There are, however, some common qualities in all these working methods. The first common feature is neutrality. All training programs stress the importance of the mediator to remain as impartial as possible. One of the reasons for the frequent recommendation of co-operation of a pair or a team of mediators is to guard against biases. However, lately, the power (im)balance between the sexes has strongly come up to the agenda of training programs.

Secondly, in all programs it is pointed out that the decision for separation, divorce or reconciliation is solely the responsibility of the partners themselves. Mediator should not make even recommendations on these. What s/he can do is to clarify the situation and act as a catalyst.

Thirdly, in many programs the role of the mediator is defined as active and directive, in contrast to e.g. such therapeutic approaches where the therapist remains passive letting the client lead the discussion.

There are (at least) four professions which each have contributed to the development of mediation with their own special expertise: the priests, the lawyers, the social workers, and the psychologists. A professional mediator very often uses a combination of the skills of the above-mentioned experts.

2.1.   Mediation (reconciliation) used for re-uniting of the spouses

The most traditional view of looking at mediation is trying to make the partners settle their disputes and start to live together again. This has especially been the case in those countries where divorce has not been available. Often, it is the priest who is given the task of negotiation and persuasion. This is realistic in situations where both partners want to settle their disputes and in cases where no actual separation has happened.

Reconciliation may also be symbolic and happen on the psychological level. Although, as stated above, most professionals do not believe in re-uniting of the spouses against their own will, often one of the partners (as well as relatives and especially children) still hope that it could be done.

For reconciliation not much training is given. It is often believed that the basic training for the clerical tasks as such should prepare the clergymen to deal with people in marital disputes. In addition, in many countries there are extra courses in marriage counselling even for ministers and their assistants.

The training to marriage counselling (including reconciliation) may include the following elements[2]:

1.   An approach to counselling

2.   The role of the mediator

3.   General information (including statistics) on contemporary marriage

4.   Phases of marriage (early, middle, later years)

5.   Social and psychological factors behind the marital breakdown

6.   Special problems (indecision, infidelity, jealousy, sexual variations, alcoholism, violence, depression)

7.   Preventing breakdown and support for marriage.

There might be separate courses and workshops for this training as well as reading lists and supervised practice with actual cases. The intensity and length of the training vary considerably.

In his foreword, the Editor of the series of The New Library of Pastoral Care Derek Blows warns, "There is always a danger that a pastor who drinks deeply at the well of a secular discipline may loose his grasp of his own pastoral identity and become 'just another' social worker or counsellor. It in no way detracts from the value of these professions to assert that the role and task of the pastor are quite unique among the helping professions and deserve to be clarified and strengthened rather than weakened...

At the same time the pastor cannot afford to work in a vacuum. He needs to be able to communicate and co-operate with those helpers in other disciplines whose work may overlap, without loss of his own unique role. This in turn will mean being able to communicate with them through some understanding of their concepts and language."[3]

2.2. Mediation as means to reach agreements upon matters arising from the breakdown

It is, however, a reality that counselling is not a process which guarantees reconciliation. Even if it would be seen as a highly desirable outcome and every effort is made to achieve it, couples may come to a mediator at a stage of irretrievable breakdown of the relationship. When it is accepted that the breakdown is final, the mediation does not aim to re-unite the partners.

A common conclusion is that reconciliation procedures have small chance of success, at least conducted through the court at the stage of separation or divorce. However, conciliation procedures at this same stage have been able to "civilise" the process of the breakdown. Conciliation therefore is used to assist the partners to deal with the consequences of the established breakdown of their marriage, whether resulting in a divorce or in a separation, by reaching agreements or giving consents or reducing the area of conflict upon custody, support, access to and education of the children, financial provision, the disposition of the matrimonial home, lawyers' fees, and every other matter arising from the breakdown which calls for a decision of future arrangements.[4]

A great deal of the area of conciliation are legal matters, and accordingly, in many countries, especially USA, there are lawyers specialised in divorce mediation. Where social workers and psychologists are practising as conciliators, lawyers often are engaged as consultants and also co-mediators to the mediation services.

Even if the main target of the conciliation is to reach an agreement, it often is not possible to make this before some kind of mutual understanding and, if not positive feelings, at least tolerance towards another is achieved between the partners. In Finland, the stages of conciliation are called 1. 'preconciliation', i.e. dealing with the conflicting objectives and marital disputes of the partners; the nature of this work is often that of crisis work, 2. 'conciliation', the phase when the actual agreements are made, and 3. 'cleaning up', supporting the family after divorce, checking the situation of the children and remedying the possible problems of the agreements.[5] Accordingly, it is not sufficient for the mediator to master the making of an agreement, s/he also needs skills for resolving underlying disputes.

The training of mediators for conciliation often follows the systems developed in USA. The training is post-gradual and the basic profession of the trainees can be e.g. solicitor, social worker, psychologist or counsellor. The usual form of the training is a series of several training courses of 2 to 14 days under a period of, for instance, two years. The training consists of workshops, exercises, reading lists, and supervision of actual mediation cases.

A typical content for a program for the training of mediators would be as follows:[6]

I Conflict Resolution Theory and Skills
The Nature of Conflict, The Adjudicatory Model, Types of Conflict, Ways of Dealing with Conflict

II Alternative Dispute Resolution
A Spectrum of Processes, The ADR Processes, Dispute Resolution Mythology

III Negotiation Theory and Skills
Competitive and Integrative Approaches, Principled Negotiation, Negotiation Power, Balance Negotiation Power, Overall Facilitative Structure

IV Being a Mediator
The Science and Art of Mediation, Roles of the Mediator, Benefits of Mediation, Comparing Business and Family Mediation, Mediation Cultures

V Getting the Mediation Started
Qualities of Mediation, Initial Contacts, Sample Letter to Clients with Appointment, Sample Client Information, Sample Agreement to Mediate, Sample Standards of Mediation Practice, Sample Pre-Emptive Letter to Legal Counsel, Letter Arranging Civil Mediation Session, The Mediator's Opening Statement, Sample Introductory Session Agenda, Sample Letter Following Initial Consultation, Suggested Ground Rules, Resolving Pressing Issues, Sample Working Session Agenda, Sample Questionnaires and Forms

VI Mediation Strategy
Mediation Approaches, The Interest-Based Option Generation Approach, The Hypothesis Generation and Testing Approach, The Doubt and Dissonance Approach, Managing Emotional/Relational Issues

VII Communication and Facilitation Skills
Introduction, Question Forms, Outcome and Evidence Questioning, Rapport Development, Indirect Techniques, An Overall Model

VIII Psychological and Emotional Issues of Divorce
Divorce Effects and Prevalence, Effects of Divorce on Children, Introduction to Family Systems Theory, Emotional Stages of Ending a Relationship, Comparing Mediation and Litigation, Typical Reactions of Children to Divorce, Signs of Stress in Children

IX Mediating Agreement on Parenting Issues
Comprehensive List of Parenting Issues, Custody Language in Mediated Agreements, Exchanging the Children, Children's Rights in Divorce, What Parents Can Do to Help Children with Divorce, Developmentally-Appropriate Parenting, Erickson's Psychosocial Developmental Stages, Time Sharing Guidelines of Robert E Adler, Talking to Children in Mediation

X Facilitating Agreement on Support
Child Support, Child Support Guidelines, Customised Child Support Calculation, Facilitating Agreement on Spousal Support, Customised

61

Calculation of Spousal Support, Statutory and Legal Standards for Determining Spousal Support

XI Facilitating Agreement on Property & Debt Issues
The Legal Context: Equity and Community Property States, Quantity and Quality Considerations, Sample Property and Debt Division Charts

XII Tax Issues Associated with Separation and Divorce
Review of Various Tax Issues, Tax Provisions Relating to Divorce

XIII Drafting the Parties' Agreement
Drafting the Parties' Agreement, Guidelines for Drafting Memoranda of Understanding, Sample Marital Settlement Agreement Provisions, Sample Memoranda of Understanding

XIV Practice and Policy Issues in Mediation
Assessing Appropriateness for Mediation of Divorce, Power, Control and Abuse, Determining Appropriateness for Mediation - Tolman Screening Model, Negotiating Ability and Safety Issues in Mediation, Alcohol and Drug Abuse Issues in Mediation, Child Abuse Issues in Mediation

XV Mediation Ethics

XVI Building a Practice and Networking

XVII National and State ADR Organisations

XVIII Legislation and Regulation
Such long training would give the trainee the licence to act as a professional mediator. However, parts of this kind of training could be useful also for such professionals who are not full-time mediators but who have to do some kinds of marital work under their own duties.

2.3. Mediation as a conflict solving method in marital conflicts, breakdown and divorce

In many countries, mediation is used as a conflict solving method in breakdown and divorce. More than merely reaching agreements, the mediation aims to solve some of the basic problems behind marital disputes.

A good example of this kind of mediation is the divorce mediation in Flanders[7].

The application of mediation as a method for solving conflicts in the field of marital conflict, marital breakdown and divorce, is still very young in Flanders and has been explored not longer than 6 years ago. The initiative to introduce divorce mediation in Flanders was taken by the Federation for Family Counselling (FCLG) Services in the early nineties after several contacts with mediation services in the different European countries, particularly the Anglo-Saxon countries where mediation has been introduced and applied since the eighties. The scientific research carried out in USA,

Canada, Australia and England showed convincing evidence of the positive perspective for mediation as a problem solving method for pre and post divorce/separation conflict. The benefits for both children and parents and the lower costs of divorces by consent for society had convinced the organisation to promote mediation and to start the formation of divorce mediators in Flanders. The changing of the divorce legislation in 1994 simplified the long procedures for divorce. In 1995, the principle of co-parenting after divorce was introduced, which helped to create a context favourable for mediation.

The federal structure of Belgium creates a discussion about whether divorce mediation should be connected to the Department of Justice (federal) and thus practised by lawyers, or connected to the Department of Welfare (Flemish Community) and operated by social workers. The proposition of law, presented in February 1998, considers mediation as a Flemish community subject. It presents a reglementation of the divorce mediation with standards for practice, formation and accreditation of both mediation services and mediators, under the jurisdiction of the Flemish Community. It includes both lawyers and professional welfare workers within welfare organisation and in private practice as mediators, yet it differentiates between them for their training and accreditation. The proposition of law has not yet been discussed by the Flemish Parliament so presently mediation and mediators are not subject to any reglementation.

However, since 1994 the Federation for Family Counselling Services has organised a two-year training and permanent supervision for mediators. The training program is yearly evaluated by the participants and subsequently modified by the training team together with mediators who already practice. Until now over 40 mediators have been trained and supervised. They register their work and turn their registrations in every year for analyses and research. They work mostly in welfare organisations, some in private practice. The Federation does not receive any financial support for the training or the development of the mediation practice. Thus, the mediation training program is dependent on the benevolence of the Institute for Communication, a training institute to give the necessary support for organising the training. Nevertheless, training courses are very popular. In marital disputes, there is a high public demand for professional mediators. In addition, in 1998, the Organisation of Lawyers started a two-week training for lawyers who want to practice mediation.

Training program for mediators was organised initially by the Federation and continued by the Institute of Communication. General information of the training is as follows.

1.   The training program for mediators is open for professionals from different backgrounds such as psychologists, solicitors, pedagogists, sociologists, social workers, and counsellors. This process proves to be a workable collaboration which highly stimulates mutual understanding and learning between the professional groups.

2.   The program is multi-disciplinary in its content and introduces insight from theory and practice in psychology, sociology and law in an

integrated way. Different mediation models are introduced with a focus on the structured negotiation and the therapeutic model. Intervention skills, process-leading skills and strategies are learned. Great emphasis is placed on the basic attitude of neutrality of the mediator. Specifically the attitude and method of the so-called multi-directed partiality is trained.

3. The training is elaborated as an experiential and methodical learning process in which the balance between knowledge, skills and attitudes is carefully assessed.

4. The mediators are trained to practice an integrative mediation model with great emphasis on the parenting aspect and a voluntary, non-court-connected mediation. Court-mandated mediation is practically non-existing in Flanders.

5. The two-year program contains 30 training days with 186 hours of courses and 69 hours of reading and reporting (a total of 255 hours). It is modelled after the highest criteria of the training programs in the different European countries and involves highly qualified and experienced trainers and supervisors.

2.4. Mediation supporting deeper understanding and personal growth of family members

In some countries, including Finland and Sweden, mediation services can be used by the family members in any kind of family problems. The basic idea is to offer services early enough so that the disputes can be dealt with more easily, and thus the mediation may possibly also prevent separation and divorce. The core issue in the family mediation in Finland is to help the situation of the children in a family conflict.

Although the purpose of the legislation is well grounded, this kind of definition of mediation has been critiqued for obscuring the role of mediation with that of marital or family therapy. Divorce mediation and family therapy may have quite different aims and working methods. In practice, however, the term mediation usually is used only in connection with divorce and separation.

The Finnish municipalities have the obligation to arrange services for mediation, but the use of the services is voluntary for the families, strictly confidential and free of charge. In different municipalities, mediation can be sought for in social welfare centres, in municipal family guidance centres, or in the family counselling centres by the Lutheran Church. When the system was started in 1989, short training courses for workers were arranged. In addition, several family guidance centres took part in a three-year project (1992-1994) by the National Research and Development Centre for Welfare and Health (STAKES). The objectives of the project were to clarify the role and organisation of mediation and to develop working methods with divorced people.

The basic qualification for the mediators is social worker, psychologists, doctor, or other person with training and experience of work

64

with families. An individual supervision is also essential. A great deal of the mediators have a two to three year training in family therapy which qualify them to family therapists. There are several organisations and universities with training programs in family therapy. The licence for therapists is granted by the National Board of Medicolegal Affairs.

In addition (or sometimes instead) mediators may have extra courses of one week in divorce mediation, in conflict resolution, or marriage counselling in general. For an experienced worker, these may be sufficient, but the newcomers would gain from a more systematic and long-lasting training. There is a need for a special training program. However, no permanent training tradition has been established especially for divorce mediation .

The one week training courses for divorce mediation have included the following:

- The theoretical frame of the training: conflict resolution (compared with e.g. crisis, developmental stage or role theories)
- Mediation in the individual working settings
- The role and function of mediation
- Different family structures and mediation
- Legal affairs in mediation
- Marriage Act
- Agreements on children
- Examples of mediation sessions (video recordings)
- Case analyses (the point of view of the mother/father)
- Children in the process of mediation
- Life changes after divorce
- The integration of social, psychological and legal work in mediation
- Division of labour between mediators and different agencies

The forms of the training have been lectures, group works, analyses of cases trough video recorded sessions, and plenum discussions. The trainees have obtained a certificate for their participation.

3.   European Master in Mediation

In response to a proposal from a number of institutions active in the field of mediation, the Institut universitaire Kurt Bösch (Sion, Valais) has worked with a team of specialists to assess the introduction of a post-graduate training qualification in mediation. There are several partner universities collaborating in the program.[8]

A course called "European Master in Mediation" will be arranged from November 1998 to December 2000.[9] Candidates for the European Masters in Mediation will normally:

- hold a university first degree giving access to postgraduate study;
- have had initial mediation training and three years' experience in conflict management,

but alternative qualifications will also be considered.

Every two years 80 candidates will be chosen for all Europe. Selection will be carried out so that each dossier will be assessed by a panel selected from the members of the European Scientific Council[10], based on the criteria drawn up by the Teaching Committee. Candidates may be invited to attend a selection interview. On satisfactory completion of the course the student will be awarded a "European Masters in Mediation" of the Institut universitaire Kurt Bösch.

The course covers both the theoretical and practical aspects and the applicable contexts of mediation, as a defined discipline and within an interdisciplinary perspective. The theoretical foundations include the analysis of conflict theory, negotiation theory and approaches to conflict management.

The course looks at various mediation practises within applicable contexts (familial, penal, social, educational, cultural, administrative, environmental, local, international politics, health), different mediation procedures within institutional structures, and the techniques used.

The aim of the course is to develop the students' ability to:

- apply their knowledge, competence, theoretical and practical skills as effective mediators
- master the negotiation and communication skills involved in mediation
- promote a global and transversal approach to mediation
- formulate and implement mediation projects
- manage, run and develop mediation services
- valorise the European dimension of mediation.

Teaching will be based on lectures on theoretical issues, reading, role-play, case studies and documentary research. Tutors will assist students in defining training programme in the light of their professional objectives. The course is organised as follows:

- individual training in the country of origin of each student, supervised by tutors and representatives of the partner institutions

- six seminars (four of one week, one of two weeks during the summer vacation, one training assessment session of one week at the end of the course) organised over a period of two years at the Institut universitaire Kurt Bösch in English and French (but the student has right to select any language to be used for individual work and assessment)

- one or more training placements abroad.

4. Conclusions and recommendations

As described above, the training of mediators is at present quite heterogeneous, as is the whole concept of mediation. Curiously enough, although the mediation itself may be statutory in a given country, even there the training of mediators is not arranged on a permanent basis, or it is left to private institutions and societies. Maybe it is too easily thought that the basic training of certain professionals would ensure them with skills suitable for mediation.

However, a new era is beginning with the "European Master in mediation"-program. It remains to be seen how well the new international and interdisciplinary training will suit the different countries. Some parts of the training are quite universal, some do not "travel" well, especially when the legislation is concerned.

As stated in the beginning, all workers who need some knowledge about family mediation do not need to specialise in it. There are several stages of training which should be available in all countries: short basic introductory courses, advanced courses, and possibility to specialise in mediation. However, on this phase of development, it is easy to agree with the recommendations of the Committee of Ministers to Member States on Family Mediation[11] that it would be premature to implement more formal requirements in this area until mediation is more widely practised at a European level.

5. References

[1]Modified from "Marriage Matters" (London 1979, p. 63), a consultative document by the Working Party on marriage guidance set up by the Home Office in consultation with the Department of Health and Social Security.
[2]The presentation follows loosely the ideas of Dr Jack Dominian, Director of Marriage Research Centre in "Make or Break. An introduction to marriage counselling" (SPCK, Holy Trinity Church, London, 1984).
[3]Ibid, pp. vii-viii.
[4]Definition by Finer Committee, referred in "Marriage Matters" p. 75.
[5]Sirpa Taskinen (1994) in preface to "En ole katkera, mutta kuitenkin... Avioerosta selviytyminen ja perheasiain neuvottelu" (I am not bitter, but still... Divorce survival and negotiation in family matters), STAKES, raportteja 166, Helsinki.
[6]See, for instance, the home pages of The Mediation Center, Eugene, Oregon, Academy of Family Mediators, http://www.to-agree.com/divtable.htm
[7]Kindly contributed by Diana Evers, Family sociologist., Coordinator and trainer of the mediator training at the Institute of Communication, Member of the Board of the European Master Degree in Mediation (Inter-university Program). Department of Sociology, Leuven.
[8]Universidad de Barcelona-Fundació Bosch i Gimpera (Barcelona), Université de Genève, Katholieke Universiteit Leuven, London School of Economics and Political Sciences, Centre de droit patrimonial de la famille (Louvain-La-Neuve), Université Lumière Lyon II, Université René Descartes (Paris), Division juridique de la Faculté de Droit et des Sciences économiques, politiques et sociales (Neuchatel) and Fern Universität Hagen.

[9]Brochure: "European Master in Mediation" published by Institut universitaire Kurt Bösch 1998. (Also in internet, http://www.ikb.vsnet.ch)
[10]The members of the European Scientific Council are: Renate Winter (Wien, chairperson), Duccio Scatolero (Torino, vice-chairperson), Benoit Bastard (Paris), Jean-Pierre Bonafé-Schmitt (Lyon), Laura Cardia-Vonèche (Genève), Jocelyne Dahan (Paris), Iago De Balanzo Sola (Barcelona), Michel Delaloye (Sion), Paolo Giulini (Milano), Maria Munné (Barcelona), Tony Peters (Barcelona), Jean-Pierre Rausis (Sion), Jean-Louis Renchon (Louvain-la-Neuve), Nathalie Riomet (Nanterre), Simon Roberts (London), Claude Rossier (Sion), Katharina Sobota (Hagen), Hubert Touzard (Paris) and Charly Zuchuat (Sion).
[11]Texts of Recommendations No. R (98) 1 of the Committee of Ministers to Member States on Family Mediation, # 36. Council of Europe. DIR/JUR (98) 4.

RELATIONSHIP BETWEEN FAMILY MEDIATION AND LEGAL PROCEEDINGS

Report presented by

Antonio FARINHA
State Attorney
Lecturer of Minor and Family Jurisdiction
Centre for Judiciary Studies,
Lisbon, Portugal

Summary

1.   Analysis of the relationship between mediation and judicial proceedings brings us back to the overall relationship between family mediation and justice, which is determined by the interplay between justice and the citizen in meeting legitimate expectations vis-à-vis protecting private and family life. This relationship also involves providing immediately effective judicial solutions in cases of family unit splits, so that parental responsibility can be jointly exercised, taking due account of all the prerequisites of personal fulfilment. This interaction forges complementary or alternative links between family mediation and justice that show the specificity of family mediation and its independence from the general judicial system.

2.   When family mediation preceed the judicial action they are more likely to succeed, as they prevent the conflict from deteriorating and establish a negotiated, consensus-based approach to the family conflicts.

        But even if judicial proceedings have already commenced, family mediation is still extremely valuable, because it forces those involved to consider the respective roles of the parties, judges, social workers and experts in relation to the legal proceedings. Deciding on the appropriate judicial channels for effective family mediation in a court context and defining the requisite scope, time limits and procedures for appointing and paying the family mediator are important criteria for preserving the dividing line between family mediation and legal proceedings.

        When assessing requests for family mediation that are submitted during legal proceedings and are aimed at imposing or amending a previous court decision, a common occurrence in custody cases, account should be taken of how genuinely the parties are interested in and intend to proceed with the mediation. The concern to avoid miscarriages of justice and expedite judicial proceedings is particularly important here.

3.   The activities and duties of the mediator and the judge, and their mutual relations, are based on both complementarity and autonomy. Harmonising and combining these two judicial and non-judicial areas of

activity involve confining the judge's role within the limits of the judiciary and adapting it to the methods, nature and aims of family mediation for the duration of the legal proceedings.

4.   The main precondition for attaining the ultimate aims of family mediation, namely concluding an agreement and agreeing on a means of communication for the future, is the confidentiality of the information submitted by the parties during the mediation procedure.   A clear explanation of confidentiality at both the substantive and procedural levels can clarify its contents and show that it depends on both the parties and the mediator. Although it cannot be absolute, confidentiality is a prerequisite for the dignity and efficiency of the whole process, which explains the importance of ensuring proper co-ordination of the judicial and non-judicial aspects.

Report

1. INTRODUCTION

1.1 Family Mediation/Justice - A complementary relationship

No one any longer seriously disputes the fact that the State only has a subsidiary, wholly complementary role to play in settling family cases involving separation and divorce, prompting an obvious trend towards dealing with such matters out of court.

The main family law aspects here are the right to respect for private and family life and the fundamental right of parents to raise and maintain their own children.

Where families do have to break up, there is now a clear legal preference for a friendly settlement of the basic family problems, if possible out of court.

This trend towards out-of-court settlements reflects the general democratisation process in society, giving the parties concerned the capacity and responsibility for settling their own problems.

This development has also been encouraged by the fact that court decisions in family cases are not usually binding. The emphasis is on efficiency rather than on abstract authority or the exemplary value of a judgment. This means replacing the model of "ritualised justice" with that of "neighbourhood justice" based on the responsible participation and interested action by the individual citizen.

From this angle, family mediation enables all the wishes and needs of the interested parties and their families to be identified and catered for, facilitating innovative solutions suited to each individual's and each family's specific situation. It also responds to and fleshes out such vague legal concepts as "the interests of the child" and "the interests of the spouse", which set the limits on "neighbourhood justice" and militate for bringing such matters out of the jurisdiction of the courts. In pursuing these aims family mediation draws on and develops the parties' capacities for communication and self-determination.

The nature, aims and methodology of family mediation facilitate and promote "neighbourly" relations between the justice system and the citizen.

This aspect is particularly important for securing a judicial definition of the exercise of parental responsibilities in situations of separation and divorce.

As we know, when families break up, there are cogent psychological, sociologic and legal reasons for advocating the joint exercise of parental responsibilities.

However, not all divorcing parents have the requisite communication skills and mutual understanding to jointly exercise their parental responsibilities as they did when married. Even when they have, if the children's interests are to be protected, ie if we are to secure the requisite conditions for them to develop harmoniously and gradually become self-reliant, as well as the interests of both parents, a consensus between the parents is obviously the optimum basis for **joint** exercise of **parental authority**.

Given that such agreement, whatever the mode of exercise of parental responsibilities, must be tailored to the actual situation and facilitate joint exercise of parental authority, it appears to be encroaching on a justice system that must consider and promote the interests of the whole family.

This is why family justice and family mediation must be complementary.

Family mediation also helps improve family justice by making judicial decisions more appropriate, expeditious and efficient and therefore reducing the courts' workload and improving their structures and mode of operation.

In this connection, comments 7, 8 and 9 of the Explanatory Memorandum of Recommendation No. R (98) 1 point to the following advantages of concluding agreements through family mediation:

- co-operative relationships can be made and maintained between divorcing parents;
- decisions taken on the basis of agreement are more likely to be complied with;
- the complexity and duration of any subsequent judicial proceedings are reduced;
- the financial costs and expenditure incurred by judicial proceedings can be cut;
- the social and psychological impact of the divorce is reduced.

On the other hand, family mediation needs the judicial system to give legal force to the results attained by ensuring that the courts confirm the agreements reached by the parties.

Obviously, unless a court decision is given on the basis of an operational judicial system, and unless this decision is duly complied with, the conditions for the exercise of freedom cannot exist. At the end of the day, family mediation depends on these conditions, as guaranteed by the judicial system.

This is further confirmation that family mediation and justice must play complementary roles.

72

1.2   Family Mediation/Justice: providing alternative and different solutions

Although divorce and separation are legal concepts, they are first and foremost personal events that give rise not only to legal interests and expectations but also to non-legal affective, emotional, material, cultural and social interests.

Therefore, no exclusively or strictly legal-cum-judicial approach can cover a family conflict in its entirety and complexity. For instance, such a narrow legal approach is powerless to deal with the conflicting non-legal aspects. Furthermore, because the legal and non-legal problems are ve.y closely linked, the legal approach stands in the way of friendly settlements and enforcement of the judicial decision.

On the socio-cultural front, judicial proceedings, whatever their actual legal nature, are based on the idea of two diametrically opposed positions, irrespective of the parties' actual interests, with one winner and one loser. This reality promotes confrontation and reduces the possibilities of dialogue and understanding between the parties on the legal conflict, thus aggravating the non-legal conflict which originated the lawsuit.

Moreover, judicial proceedings are an obstacle to active, direct involvement by the parties in solving their family problems: their representatives conduct the procedural action, lawyers, advisers and experts take charge of information and communication, and judges give the decisions.

The highly-charged atmosphere of conflict that prevails in such cases and the fact that the parties concerned are only distantly involved in the decision-making process clearly show why the solutions emerging are so precarious.

Against such a background, family mediation in cases of divorce and separation provides an autonomous, fresh and innovative approach to family disputes. It constitutes a structured, informal and flexible process whose main feature is voluntary involvement by the parties concerned and their active and direct participation in identifying their own individual and shared interests and agreeing on mutually satisfactory solutions. In pursuing this aim, the parties are granted impartial, objective and confidential assistance by a qualified expert.

Family mediation is geared to re-establishing and reinforcing communication between the parties and developing their negotiating skills through proper handling of the relevant information and consideration of the available options for satisfying all the main wishes, needs and interests. Family mediation accordingly encourages intensive communication between the parties, embracing all the factors conducive to agreement and creative solutions. This approach inevitably helps the parties overcome and settle their conflict, assigning them the responsibility for securing a satisfactory solution to the problem and complying with the agreements reached.

73

This method, which is simultaneously complementary and alternative, demonstrates that the nature, methods and purposes of family mediation do indeed distinguish it from judicial proceedings. Furthermore, it can be initiated at various points in proceedings, ie before, during or after the legal action.

2. INITIATING THE FAMILY MEDIATION PROCEDURE

2.1 Family mediation prior to legal proceedings

When family mediation precedes legal action, it is not directly aimed at preventing recourse to the courts, as would be the case if the two procedures were mutually exclusive rather than complementary.

Legal proceedings are justified if the parties cannot, or will not, settle the conflict themselves and a judge is therefore needed.

The primary purpose of family mediation is to enable the opposing parties to reach a proper, satisfactory agreement. If they are unable of reluctant to settle the dispute themselves, they can secure a judicial settlement.

Initiating family mediation in a completely non-judicial context seems to make it easier for all the parties to become genuinely involved in the procedure. Such mediation also has the advantage of providing a climate of informal exchange and facilitating a broader range of communication and more flexible discussion. The parties' real interests have not yet frozen into adamant procedural positions, and so this danger can be avoided. There are no time limits on mediation, making it easier to try out proposed agreements and tailor them to realities. In this context, the law is a mere reference point and a means of ultimately validating the agreement and consolidating the parties' wishes, which is a positive contribution to the image of the judicial system in society.

The parties freely determine the scope of such mediation. However, since the personal and property issues raised by divorce cases are independent *de facto*, and in order to prevent future conflicts, it is advisable to make it as comprehensive as possible. This enables any disputes regarding parental authority, division of property and payment of maintenance to be settled simultaneously.

Given the importance of dealing with all these aspects when concluding an agreement to the satisfaction of all the parties, the mediator should endeavour to identify all the relevant issues during the mediation procedure. Parties must also be provided with all the necessary information for the legal validity and enforcement of the agreement reached.

Moreover, prior family mediation is useful even in the event of mutual consent to legal proceedings in cases relating to divorce, separation or joint parental authority. Divorce is a painful procedure from the affective, emotional, psychological, family, social and economic angles and the parties usually want to get it over with as quickly as possible, often without properly considering their vital wishes, needs and interests. The fact that some types of proceedings do not require litigants to have a lawyer and that both parties can be represented by a single lawyer in other types prevents them from properly considering the vital issues or their basic interests. In such cases, since judges are not in possession of the requisite factual information, they can only endeavour to identify settlements that are blatantly improper or unfair.

This frequently leads to infringements of the agreements and the consequent legal decisions, with consequent proceedings brought to modify the previous arrangements. This is detrimental to the child's behaviour and development, communication between the parents and the joint exercise of parental authority.

The advantages of initiating family mediation prior to legal proceedings are such that special efforts should be made to advertise it and make it generally accessible. Some countries have introduced procedures to give couples with children immediate recourse to mediation or to require that they attend free personal information sessions on family mediation, before any proceedings are commenced. This has proved very effective in changing the traditional cultural approaches to family conflicts, making family mediation more efficient and simplifying judicial procedures.

Since couples frequently exploit their own children to promote their side of the conflict, and since the higher interests of children must be safeguarded in proceedings involving them, mediation must be made available not only for divorce proceedings but also for all cases concerning the exercise of parental responsibilities.

The guarantee of access to family mediation could consist of either a specific number of free sessions, free legal aid or some other similar type of assistance. When it precedes legal proceedings, information must be coherently provided on all available non-judicial remedies. How can this be done where family mediation is only recognised and provided, within a judicial context, after the commencement of legal proceedings? Should the guarantee of access to family mediation also cover the period before the judicial action?

We might quote the case of a pilot project introduced at the end of 1997 under the auspices of the Portuguese Minister of Justice. This project is currently being implemented and is aimed at providing family mediation as a public service in divorce and separation cases, to deal with various aspects of inter-parental conflict, ie disputes as to the exercise of parental responsibilities.

The department responsible for providing this service answers queries from the general public, conducts family mediation and endeavours to encourage its use.

In answering queries the department attempts to provide information on the family mediation procedure, analyse its relevance to the specific case and take the drama out of the family break-up by appealing to the parents' ability to re-define their own parental function. The main aim is to talk, either individually or together, to both the parents involved in the separation, establish contacts with professionals from the legal and psychosocial fields and provide media information.

The initiation and continuation of any family mediation procedure is caracterised by the fact that it is completely voluntary and free of charge.

The department concentrates on pre-judicial action, operating out of court in order to guarantee the parties' freedom of determination. In other words, the courts have no say in initiating, organising or operating the mediation process.

The service is widely publicised in order to promote an atmosphere of give-and-take, enabling family conflicts to be settled on a friendly basis, by organising colloquies and debates and preparing and disseminating the relevant information.

These aims and strategies prioritise family mediation prior to legal proceedings, promoting a social atmosphere of dialogue which places the responsibility on the parties themselves, the community leaders and institutions and the media.

2.2   Family mediation conducted during legal proceedings

Court intervention in settling family disputes remains subsidiary as long as agreement between the parties is still possible. Family mediation is, therefore, still an option even during legal proceedings.

It is agreed that family mediation can take place at any stage in proceedings, whatever the level of **jurisdiction.** The aim is to seek consensus in settling family disputes, whether during judicial investigations, the actual trial, or even possible appeal proceedings.

However, should family mediation be admitted only in proceedings in which both parties are to be heard? The answer has to be no, because in cases involving the inalienable rights and interests of minors as the primary criteria for the judicial decision it is immaterial whether the parties appear or not.

Family mediation is aimed at securing an agreement between the parties, which presupposes their willingness to establish proper communication and exchange information. This means that their involvement in the mediation process must be voluntary, whether it be initiated by the judge or by the parties themselves.

Judges are particularly well placed to decide whether family mediation would be useful in any given case. In particular, they can explain to the parties the limits of the court's action during discussions and attempts at conciliation, where they act as third parties persuading the parties to settle their own differences. If the parties are assigned basic responsibility for pursuing their various interests and their self-actualisation as persons and parents (though obviously avoiding denying justice) by involving them closely in the definition of acceptable solutions, they can hardly fail to understand the importance of a friendly settlement. Judges must accordingly have, and transmit to the parties concerned, a full grasp of the family conflicts arising out of divorce and separation and positively refocus the conflict, emphasising the parties' ability to overcome it satisfactorily. They must also encourage the parties to replace any unrealistic ideas of an all-powerful judicial system with an awareness of the actual scope and limitations of judicial settlements of family disputes.

If family mediation is to remain autonomous from legal proceedings, judges must base the corresponding decision on the parties' free and informed consent to such mediation, establishing a non-judicial type of communication in order to settle the dispute. The mediation procedure necessitates a stay of proceedings and the confirmation of the parties' consent during the initial stages. Such confirmation is vital to ensure that their participation remains voluntary and prevent them feeling any constraints in the judicial environment.

The parties, who are the decisive participants in both the mediation and judicial procedures, must obviously be empowered to initiate the family mediation by agreeing to a stay of the proceedings. The judge's role should be confined to taking urgent decisions and preventing any miscarriage of justice, particularly if there have been prior judicial proceedings.

In all such situations the resumption of proceedings must be a matter exclusively for the parties, whether individually or jointly, in order to guarantee the right of access to justice and the courts. Proceedings must in all cases resume by the end of the period stipulated for the stay.

It is important to consider other ways of promoting mediation during judicial proceedings as a means of securing friendly settlements of family conflicts. We might, for example, envisage the possibility of distributing information documents to the parties on family mediation after the commencement of the legal action or the serving of the summons to appear in court. Again, lawyers might be required to provide their clients, whatever their procedural status, with information on mediation services, especially in proceedings relating to parental authority and divorce when under-age children are involved. The same requirement could be imposed on the technical staff involved in the proceedings (social workers and experts), so that the parties could consider whether family mediation would be appropriate in their particular case.

Family mediation must therefore be included in the training of such technical staff, as well as in that of judges and lawyers.

Involvement by lawyers in the mediation process leads us to the question of the role of the "lawyer/mediator". This highly complex issue concerning the exercise of two different functions by the same person has not yet been satisfactorily settled. Should lawyers trained in family mediation be allowed to offer to mediate for their clients and thus simultaneously act as lawyers and mediators? And should a mediator who is also a lawyer be able to conduct family mediation while also acting as a lawyer to provide the parties with the necessary legal information and ultimately drafting the legally prescribed agreement? Why not enrich the family mediation process with a legal expert who, besides his training and skills in family mediation, can provide the parties with legal information and couch the agreement in the appropriate legal terms for its confirmation by the court? Why not use this means of bringing the judicial and mediation systems closer together, with the advantage of opening up the legal and judicial systems and making them more flexible? Or, on the contrary, would merging both functions in the same person distort the mediation procedure by depriving it of its status as an independent means of conflict settlement and basically subjecting its substance to the judiciary? Would mediators be compromising their neutrality by acting as lawyer, ie as experts in legal and judicial matters? If they had this dual status, how could we prevent them from controlling not only the mediation procedure but also its actual substance? Can we deprive the parties to the mediation procedure of legal advice and help from other lawyers and legal experts?

While a stay of proceedings is apparently a precondition for guaranteeing the autonomy of family mediation, other elements may also influence it.

Let us begin with the scope of family mediation. Must such mediation necessarily be confined to judicial disputes? By linking mediation up to part or all of the case as submitted to the court, will we not be altering its nature and autonomy, given that mediation consists of nothing more than the consideration of the whole family conflict and of all the parties' interests? We must remember here that the judicial approach to family conflicts invariably distinguishes between the different types of proceedings, and disregards any interrelations between their component parts, be they personal, pecuniary, parental or conjugal. Furthermore, the parties take no such compartmentalised view of their conflict, and seem to be more satisfied and suffer less in financial terms where the mediation is comprehensive in scope. Comprehensive mediation is better suited to settling the legal dispute and finding a harmonious solution to all aspects of the family conflict, thereby preventing any future litigation.

Let us deal secondly with the question of time limits on family mediation. In order to protect the autonomy of the mediation procedure, flexible time limits are needed so that the process can be adapted to the time available to each party. A simple agreement between the parties is usually sufficient to draw up a suitable schedule for the procedure and prevent any miscarriages of justice.

Thirdly, the selection and appointment of the mediator can affect the autonomy of family mediation procedures conducted during legal proceedings. Initiating family mediation means transferring from the judicial to the non-judicial sphere, returning to square one, the situation preceding the judicial proceedings, and restoring the full capacity of the parties to manage their own interests. Does this mean that they should have primary responsibility for selecting and appointing their own mediator? Should the court act only if the parties fail to do so? And, if so, should the judge's role be confined to suggesting a reputable mediation institute to take charge of the specific mediation procedure? Should the court exercise its powers solely within the limits of the judicial environment?

Lastly, what should be the level and mode of payment of the family mediator? Family mediation is conducted in an environment of very delicate interpersonal relations based on trust, which mainly necessitates empathy, active listening and mutual respect between the parties and the mediator. Are the determination of a fee by the mediator and his or her direct payment by the parties a condition and essential features of mediation? Are the simplicity and efficiency of this system in greater conformity with the very nature and autonomy of family mediation than the remuneration and payment effected within the judicial proceedings?

In the above-mentioned Portuguese project, family mediation can only be conducted while legal proceedings are pending after a voluntary stay of proceedings, decided under an agreement concluded between the parties in accordance with the law.

Mediation is conducted by interdisciplinary teams of lawyers, psychologists and social workers specially trained in the field of family mediation.

This project is basically extra-judicial, but it provides for supplying the additional information required for court confirmation of any agreements concluded.

2.3   Family mediation following legal proceedings

Whenever compulsory action is deemed necessary, judicial proceedings are the optimum means of settling the dispute. This fact is particular obvious when family mediation follows a set of judicial proceedings.

In such cases the family conflicts to be mediated should be strictly selected in order to avoid the risks of impracticable mediation procedures and miscarriages of justice. Particular care should be taken with situations in which mediation would be inappropriate because of a previously ascertained power imbalance between the parties. This applies to cases of serious domestic violence and child abuse, drug addiction and psychological disorders or mental illness.

It is also important to realise when the parties are deliberately delaying their compliance with judicial decisions and possibly obstructing the protection of the interests of third parties, especially of their children, and the proper administration of justice.

The judge should therefore be provided with assistance and any other measures deemed necessary to assess the relevance and appropriateness of mediation. Similarly, **particular stress should be laid on consent at the beginning of the mediation process.**

Special consideration should be given to keeping the mediation process as short as possible, as the stay of proceedings should not normally be overly protracted.

In the Portuguese pilot project, when family mediation follows judicial proceedings it is aimed at preventing infringements of agreements on the exercise of parental responsibilities, facilitating agreed reviews of such agreements, ensuring continuous parent-child relations and encouraging joint exercise of parental authority.

The project provides for organising mutual assistance groups and holding colloquies and discussions as a means of monitoring progress.

3. THE MEDIATOR/JUDGE RELATIONSHIP AND THE JUDGE'S POWERS

The judge's direct or indirect power to appoint the family mediator is naturally subject to general suitability requirements and specific conditions vis-à-vis training and qualifications, as well as circumstances disqualifying the judge or impeding the exercise of the functions in question.

Most cases of disqualification concern the exercise of activities incompatible with the independence of the office of mediator.

Impediments, on the other hand, concern personal and family relations which the mediator and situations in which he or she has a professional or procedural interest.

Consideration must also be given to situations preventing mediators appointed from exercising their functions and provision made to enable them to stand down. Such situations concern non-compliance with the rules governing the mediation procedure or challenges to the mediator's impartiality, where it can reasonably be assumed that if the mediator continues to direct the procedure the parties will have difficulty reaching an autonomous decision.

In such situations the judge is empowered to discontinue the mediator's mandate, at his or her own request, or even to terminate the whole mediation process if the mediator considers it to be jeopardised. However, since the information supplied by mediators is subject to the obligation to maintain confidentiality, they cannot disclose the exact reasons why they were requested to stand down or why the mediation procedure was terminated. This restricts the judge's discretionary powers. Does this mean that the judicial decision should be based on the request to terminate the mediator's mandate as assessed by an independent ethical body? Could such an approach safeguard the autonomy of mediation without adversely affecting the legal proceedings?

Where the mediation procedure is conducted while legal proceedings are pending and the mediator has been appointed by the court, he or she should inform the latter as soon as it becomes obvious that mediation is impracticable, so as to prevent the adverse effects of delays in the administration of justice. If an agreement is concluded between the parties, the mediator must inform the court of this fact at the end of the period of suspension of proceedings.

Should the mediator apprise the judge of any difficulties arising during the mediation process?

Mediators are by definition responsible for conducting and controlling mediation. They must create a climate conducive to communication and information exchange between the parties, striking a balance between their opposing positions so that they can freely negotiate their own interests with an eye to a mutual agreement. Controlling the mediation procedure presupposes controlling and overcoming any difficulties. If the problems prove insuperable, the available options are terminating the mediation procedure or relieving the mediator of his/her duties and possibly replacing him/her. Since mediation is voluntarily initiated and terminated by the parties, it is incompatible with any interventionist approach that would contradict the mediator's endeavours during the procedure to develop satisfactory bilateral communication between the parties. The judge's only role vis-à-vis any internal difficulties encountered during the mediation procedure is to assess them during the final hearing.

Ultimately, this issue brings us back to that of ensuring justice in the mediation context, which breaks down into two different aspects: justice of the procedure and justice of the results. The former essentially depends on the balance of power between the parties, the neutrality of the mediator, the self-determination of the parties (ensuring that the mediator does not exert any undue pressure or impose his or her own moral standards) and the consideration of the child's interests. The latter depends on compliance with the rules (not only legal ones) established by the parties themselves and generally corresponds to their own conception of justice.

The justice of the procedure is also conditioned by the context, essence and nature of family mediation. It must be guaranteed by the mediator's standard of professional training and qualification and compulsory compliance with the code of ethics in connection with the parties' freedom and equality in participation and decision-making. The justice of the results, on the other hand, is ensured by providing legal advice throughout the mediation procedure, and by the judge's decision either to confirmed or reject the agreement on completion of the procedure. The justice of mediation basically brings us back to the initial complementarity of mediation and justice.

Another problem arises when the court has to take emergency decisions to protect the parties, their children or their property.

In the course, usually at the beginning, of a family mediation procedure, a diagnosis is effected of any urgent problems and the expediency of a preliminary agreement to meet the parties' immediate needs in order to remove any obstacles to mediation. If one of the parties is placed in a difficult bargaining position he or she might be forced to make concessions in order to meet the said immediate needs, which would obstruct a fair settlement.

In deciding whether or not to conclude a preliminary agreement, consideration must be given to any urgent problems, possible areas of consensus or disagreement and lastly, major clashes on any of the urgent problems. Such clashes include problems that call for court intervention and a judicial decision during the stay of proceedings, with a view to preventing irreparable damage.

The first step, therefore, in ensuring compatibility between judicial intervention and family mediation is to submit any disagreements that have not been provisionally settled under a preliminary agreement to the court for a decision. It is primarily a matter for the mediator to maintain this judicial link by providing the parties with the information they need to understand the specific purpose and nature each type of intervention.

In the family mediation context the preliminary agreement is provisional, and its clauses can be altered at the request of the parties concerned as their views change during the mediation procedure. The effects of the impetus of family mediation on the terms of the preliminary agreement should also be considered in any urgent judicial decisions given, ie provision must be made for amending the latter either at the parties' request or when the circumstances of the case change.

The preliminary agreement is geared to meeting urgent needs in the most appropriate manner possible for the family in particular and the parties in general. It can be either rather flexible and general or else more structured and specific, depending on the direction taken by the procedure and the urgent needs to be met. This is why courts should also tailor their urgent judicial decisions to the requirements of individual family backgrounds.

The ultimate aim of mediation is, as we know, to enable the parties to reach a mutually satisfactory agreement, and in fact the decision to stay judicial proceedings with a view to family mediation has exactly the same objective. The court should also bear this aim in mind when giving urgent decisions, so that the judicial intervention can be dovetailed combined with the family mediation procedure. This means that the judicial decision should also give precedence to the agreed resolution of urgent problems, in this case through inter-party conciliation rather than mediation.

Once the agreement is drafted, it is for the parties to apply for its confirmation by the court, and appropriate legal advice must be provided to this end.

We should perhaps consider some aspects of the judge's power to confirm or reject the agreement.

The agreement can cover matters over which the judge has no jurisdiction *ratione materiae*. The question might also arise of the lawfulness of specific clauses in the agreement, its compliance with the parties' wishes, or even the appropriateness of certain agreed solutions for pursuing the interests at issue. Such considerations might prevent the court from confirming the agreement and hamper a friendly settlement of the judicial dispute. On the other hand, this risk can be obviated by voluntarily submitting the agreement to a court for assessment with a view to its judicial confirmation, as this enables the judge to investigate the situation and thus give a fairer decision. Therefore, whenever this voluntary measure is applied, any necessary information can be collated, the parties heard individually and meetings held between them, with a view to confirming, or possibly re-drafting, the agreement submitted. Such a measure basically provides for a smooth transition from the extra-judicial to the judicial environment.

4.   CONFIDENTIALITY

The main factor in ensuring the parties' freedom and ability to take decisions, which are essential features of family mediation, is their trust in the procedure. This can be built up by the confidentiality of the procedure, which encourages their *bona fide* participation and co-operation.

Confidentiality is reflected in the secrecy of the discussions held during the family mediation procedure and the prohibition on disclosure by the mediator of any information obtained by this means. It covers the contents of the mediation sessions, interviews, and documents and dossiers filed with a view to preparing the sessions. The obligation on mediators to maintain confidentiality also covers the individuals' identities and all the facts which they know about their private lives; it extends to everything the mediator sees, hears and understands in the exercise of his or her duties.

As stipulated in Principle III.vi. of Recommendation No. R (98) 1, the professional secrecy of mediation does not apply where the parties authorise its withdrawal and in those cases allowed by national law.

If the parties so agree, the confidentiality of information filed orally or in documentary form can be extended to prevent it from being produced in evidence in any subsequent judicial proceedings. This "privilege" prevents mediators from giving evidence in such proceedings, unless the parties agree to exempt them from this prohibition. The fact is that this "privilege" belongs to the parties jointly, not to the mediator or the process, as stated in Comment 41 of the Explanatory Memorandum to the same Recommendation.

Are mediators who have been released from their obligation to maintain confidentiality entitled to refuse to give evidence? This issue must be settled by national law, which governs recognition and regulation of the mediator's obligation to maintain confidentiality. From the ethical point of view, the legal provisions on this matter in the various codes of good practice are neither clear nor uniform. Some of them require mediators to maintain confidentiality in relation to third parties and stipulate that this requirement can only be lifted if jointly agreed by the parties. Other codes impose an absolute obligation of secrecy on mediators and stipulate that this obligation can only be waived in accordance with the written consent of all the parties, including the mediators themselves. In addressing this question, should we take account of the fact that the parties control the contents of the mediation process, ie the information on which the communication and negotiation is based, and that the mediator only controls the procedure, ie the methods of ascertaining, managing and evaluating the information? This would mean that the parties should be able to mutually agree to using their own information, which they have themselves generated and exchanged during the mediation, outside this process. Should the circumstances under which the information was generated during the family mediation process entitle the mediator to restrict the use of such information? Does not the use of the family mediation process in a way or to ends unrelated or contrary to the process itself justify the mediator officially opposing any ulterior use of the information obtained therein? Is the fact that family mediation was possibly used maliciously or with illegal, immoral or obviously unfair intent a legitimate ground for such opposition?

Confidentiality is not absolute, which is why the parties must be given clear information about its limits right at the beginning of the process. Situations of child abuse and domestic violence, etc, set limits on the confidentiality and justify a consequent interruption or termination of family mediation. In the former case, the best interests of the child militate for empowering mediators to report the situation to the concerned bodies or authorities, whenever he or she has reasonable grounds to believe that the child is suffering serious abuse or neglect, as defined by law. In the latter case, if the person committing the violence fails to acknowledge and discontinue his/her acts, or if no appropriate measures are taken to ensure the victim's safety (eg judicial protection orders, provisional allocation of family residence, arranging for parents to visit their children on neutral ground), the victims and the relevant authorities must be made aware of the danger to the integrity of the person concerned, ie any credible and probable threat of imminent death or serious injury, and the mediation procedure must be terminated.

However, any reports which the mediator has to submit to the judicial authority must respect the confidentiality of the mediation process. If the mediator were empowered to advise the judge how best to decide in cases where no agreement has been reached, such a power might be used to exert pressure on the parties to reach an agreement, possibly against their wishes. The failure to respect confidentiality in such cases would result in jeopardising the mediator's impartiality and neutrality and the parties' right of negotiation and decision-making.

Bibliographical References

American Bar Association, Family Law Section Task Force (1997) *Proposed Standards of Practice for Lawyers who Conduct Divorce and Family Mediation* www.mediate.com/ethics/abafamstds.cfm

Armas, M.S.J. e Duran, A.M.S. (1995) *Aspectos Jurídicos de la Mediación Familiar*, in Ciclo de Seminários (Madrid, A.I.E.E.F.).

Babu, A./ Biletta, I./ Bonnoure-Aufiere, P./ David-Jougneau, M./ Ditchev, S./ Girot, A. et Mariller, N. (1997) *Médiation Familiale: regards croisés et perspectives* (Ramonville Saint-Agne, Editions Erès).

Bonafe-Schmitt, J-P. (1991) *Contentieux Familial et Médiation - Une Comparaison Internationale,* Disputes and Litigation (Blankenburg / Comaille & Galanter).

Bridge, C. (1996) *Conciliation and the New Zeland Family Court: Lessons for English Law Reformers,* Legal Studies, V.16, nº13, pp. 298-324.

Bustelo, D. (1995) *La Mediación Familiar Interdisciplinária* (Madrid, B.M.S. Ediciones S.L.).

Cardenas, E.J. (1995) *Un Intento de Mediación Entre Dos Viejos Enemigos: La Mediación Familiar y la Justicia de Família,* 1ª Conferência del Foro Mondial de Mediación, Madrid.

Cornelius, H. e Faire, S. (1995) *Tú Ganas, Yo Gano* (Madrid, Gaia Ediciones).

Dolto, F. (1988) *Quand les parents se séparent* (Paris, Éditions du Seuil).

Epifânio, R. e Farinha, A. (1997) *Organização Tutelar de Menores, Contributo Para Uma Visão Interdisciplinar do Direito de Menores e da Família* (Coimbra, Livraria Almedina).

Estatísticas da Justiça - Ministério da Justiça / Gabinete de Estudos e Planeamento, (1992/ 1997), Lisboa.

Farinha, A. e Lavadinho, C. (1997) *Mediação Familiar e Responsabilidades Parentais* (Coimbra, Livraria Almedina).

Fisher, R./ Ury, W. e Patton, B. (1995) *Si...de acuerdo* (Grupo Edit. Norma).

Friedman, J.D., G.J. (1993) *A Guide To Divorce Mediation* (New York, Workman Publishing Company, Inc.).

Genet, L. (1997) *Relever le défi de la médiation familiale?* Journal du Droit des Jeunes nº163.

Harvey, L.A. (1997) *The Dual Role of Evaluative Mediation* Mediation Association of Kentucky Newsletter, August.

Haynes, J.M. (1995) *Fundamentos de la Mediación Familiar* (Madrid, Gaia Ediciones).

Laurent-Boyer, L. (1998) *La Médiation Familiale - collectif multidisciplinaire coordonné par* (Québec, Les Éditions Blais Inc.).

Martins, S. (1985) *Processo e Direito Processual*, (Coimbra, Centelha).

Mcewen, C. A./ Rogers, N. H. and Maiman, R.J. (1995) *Bring in the Lawyers: Challenging the Dominant Approaches to Ensuring Fairness in Divorce Mediation* Minnesota Law Review, V.79, nº6, pp.1317-1411.

Pluyette, G. (1997) *Principes et Applications Récentes des Décrets des 22 Juillet et 13 Décembre 1996 sur la Conciliation et la Médiation Judiciaires,* Revue de l'arbitrage, nº4.

Salzberg, B. (1992) *Los Niños No Se Divorcian* (Barcelona, Logos Clínica Psicoanalítica).

Sottomayor, M.C. (1995) *Exercício do Poder Paternal relativamente à Pessoa do Filho após o Divórcio ou a Separação Judicial de Pessoas e Bens* (Porto, Universidade Católica Portuguesa - Editora).

Sullerot E. (1993) *Que Pais? Que Filhos?*, (Lisboa, Relógio D'Água).

Wallerstein, J. and Kelly, J. (1980) *Surviving the Break-up: How Children and Parents Cope with Divorce (Basic Books).*

THE STATUS OF MEDIATED AGREEMENTS
AND THEIR IMPLEMENTATION

Report presented by

Mary LLOYD
Service Co-ordinator
Family Mediation Service
Dublin, Ireland

Summary

States should facilitate the approval of Mediated Agreements by a judicial authority or other competent authority where parties request it and provide mechanisms for enforcement of such approved agreements according to national law.

*

*

This Report will deal with the subject matter of "Status of Mediated Agreements and their implementation". Firstly, as it currently stands in the Irish context as this is where the Rapporteur's greatest experience of the issue lies. The Report will go on to refer to the status of Mediated Agreements in those Member States that the Rapporteur has been able to make contact with and as reported to her by the relevant authorities from those States. The Report will also refer to the preliminary report on the Questionnaire on Family Mediation by the Working Party on Mediation and other Processes to Resolve Family Disputes (CJ-FA-GT2).

To set the stage for where Mediated Agreements stand in Ireland this Report will summarise the structure of the Family Mediation Service (FMS) in Ireland. The autonomy of mediation in Ireland. The role of the Mediator's Institute Ireland (M.I.I.). The status of the Legal Separation Agreement in Family Law. The recommendation of the Law Reform Commission in their Report on Family Courts on the application to have the Agreement recorded or made a Rule of Court. And, finally, the status of Mediated Agreements in Norway, England, Wales and Scotland as understood by the Rapporteur from discussion with authorities in these countries and as answered in the Questionnaire above.

Report

States should facilitate the approval of Mediated Agreements by a judicial authority or other competent authority where parties request it and provide mechanisms for enforcement of such approved agreements, according to national law.

1.   Introduction

This Report will deal with the subject matter of "Status of Mediated Agreements and their implementation". Firstly, as it currently stands in the Irish context as this is where the Rapporteur's greatest experience of the issue lies. The Report will go on to refer to the status of Mediated Agreements in those Member States that the Rapporteur has been able to make contact with and as reported to her by the relevant authorities from those States. The Report will also refer to the preliminary report on the Questionnaire on Family Mediation by the Working Party on Mediation and other Processes to Resolve Family Disputes (CJ-FA-GT2).

To set the stage for where Mediated Agreements stand in Ireland this Report will summarise the structure of the Family Mediation Service (FMS) in Ireland. The autonomy of mediation in Ireland. The role of the Mediator's Institute Ireland (M.I.I.) The status of the Legal Separation Agreement in Family Law. The recommendation of the Law Reform Commission in their Report on Family Courts on the application to have the Agreement recorded or made a Rule of Court. And, finally, the status of Mediated Agreements in Norway, England, Wales and Scotland as understood by the Rapporteur from discussion with authorities in these countries and as answered in the Questionnaire above.

There has been a State service of Family Mediation in Ireland since September 1986. This service is fully funded by the Irish Government and is currently under the remit of The Department of Social, Community and Family Affairs. It is a free service to the public. It is a service for marital and non-marital couples. Couples are offered up to six sessions of one hour each. Since its inception the model of mediation practised in Ireland is comprehensive mediation - in other words - all issues. This has proved to be a very enlightened approach in the practice of mediation. Mediation in Ireland is a voluntary process. The Family Mediation Service has had total autonomy in the way which mediation is practised and the standards it has adopted. Its budget was trebled in 1998 in order to expand the service nationwide.

Each year from October to May FMS runs an in-service specialist training programme in Family Mediation. We take 6 to 7 trainees. At the end of training the trainee's supervisor signs off the M.I.I. Accreditation Journal provided the trainee has reached the required standard. The Mediator's Institute Ireland (M.I.I.) is the umbrella organisation for mediators which sets the standards for practice as mediators. It accredits practitioner members. It also accredits training programmes in mediation. The training policy is set out in Policy Document No. (1) 1995 entitled The Accreditation of Professional Mediators in Ireland. The standards set by M.I.I. are recognised by our

Government Department so that in advertising for the post of Mediators for employment within the Family Mediation Service and for the posts of Service Co-Ordinator and Area Co-Ordinator applicants require M.I.I. qualifications.

In reply to a question raised in the Irish Parliament – The Dail - the then Minister responsible for FMS replied "----- I am unable to agree that it is the function of my Department or of the Family Mediation Service to establish a National Register of persons who are deemed to be qualified to practice as Family Mediators". So while there is no Government input into establishing a Register of Family Mediators, which by implication would entail looking at the standards, the development of standards has been left to M.I.I. who have established a Register. In Ireland, in addition to the Family Mediation Service there are a number of other organisations which have a mediation practice. There are a number of mediators in private practices. As mentioned already, Comprehensive Mediation is practised in Ireland. The usual issues that couples want to discuss and reach agreement on are:-

1. Parenting arrangements of their children and the circumstances under which these will be reviewed.

2. Financial Arrangements and how each of the spouses and their children will be provided for, the circumstances under which their financial arrangements will be reviewed.

3. The matrimonial home, what will happen to this, where each of the spouses and their children will live.

4. Other assets i.e. property, shares, bank accounts etc.

5. Debts/liabilities - how these will be managed and by whom.

6. Insurance policies - whether they will be retained and for whose benefit.

7. Taxation - how the couple will be taxed in a separated situation.

8. Succession Rights - and whether to retain or renounce.

9. Details of each of the spouses pension schemes and whether there is a pension in favour of the non-member spouse.

10. Whether they intend having the Mediated Agreement drawn up into a Legal Separation or intend applying for a Divorce.

FMS has drawn up Standard Clauses for the "Note of a Mediated Agreement". The heading and Preamble in the Standard Clauses are used in every Mediated Agreement prepared by FMS, which is as follows:-

Ref.:
Date of Agreement:

NOTE OF MEDIATED AGREEMENT

Between: Name & Address - Husband **and**:   Name & Address - Wife

We have arrived at the following agreements in the process of mediation.

1.   PREAMBLE

1.1   These agreements represent a total package carefully balancing our mutual and individual interests.

1.2   We have mediated this Agreement with the help of a mediator being fully aware that his/her role is to assist us in negotiating our own Agreement and not to advise us on legal or other issues.

1.3   (a)   Having taken/not taken legal advice we each take full responsibility for all decisions set out in this Agreement

(b)   Having taken/not taken legal advice neither of us intends this Agreement to be legally binding on the other unless and until it is either:

(i)   Incorporated into a Legal Separation Agreement and signed by each of us.

(ii)   Made a Consent Order of Court under the Judicial Separation Act, 1989.

(iii)   Made a Consent Order of Court under the Family Law (Divorce) Act, 1996.

(iv)   Made a Rule of Court under the Family Law (Maintenance of Spouses and Childrens Act, 1976).

1.4   We agree that *****'s solicitor, Name of Solicitor, will draw up a legal Agreement with *****'s solicitor, Name of Solicitor, approving it.

Our legal costs to be met as follows:-

1.5   It has been a precondition of the mediator's assisting us that the mediation sessions have been conducted without prejudice and that any information disclosed by either of us in our negotiations with each other is confidential.

1.6   Our Agreement is being concluded following (number) mediation sessions. Our Mediator is (Name) of the Family Mediation Service.

1.7   We married each other on the (date), in (Church, Registry Office, Place e.g. Dublin).

- - - - - - - - - - - -

As can be seen, the Mediated Agreement states whether the couple have each taken legal advice or not. We find that most couples have taken legal advice before coming to mediation. If they haven't FMS encourages separating couples to be advised by a family lawyer (solicitor) either during mediation or at the end of mediation.

When all issues are agreed by the couple, the mediator draws up the Mediated Agreement, a copy of which is sent to each spouse/partner. The Mediated Agreement is not signed by the mediator.

We find that many couples who return to re-negotiate aspects of their Mediated Agreement, sometimes many years later, have simply acted on their Mediated Agreement until such time as they decide to formalise it either by way of Legal Separation Agreement or have it made a Rule of Court or by applying for a Divorce.

In Ireland, one of the reasons why couples may decide to have their Mediated Agreement drawn up into a Legal Separation Agreement is in order to satisfy a lending institution such as a bank or building society if they are seeking a second mortgage to purchase a second home. Lending institutions ask for sight of the clause in a Legal Separation Agreement relating to property arrangements.

Also, under our tax law, where couples separate by way of Legal Separation Agreement they can elect in writing to the Revenue to continue to be jointly assessed for income tax or they may decide to opt for single assessment.

The Courts in Ireland have always held the view that the status of an agreement entered into voluntarily between a husband and wife should not be interfered with by the Court. Where a Court is asked to make an agreement a Rule of Court, the Court would enquire whether the parties were satisfied with the terms and look at the financial arrangements and the arrangements made around the children. There are two issues which can always be reviewed under Irish Family Law:

1.   Any issue in relation to children;

2.   Maintenance issues.

So there is no clean break or full and final settlement of financial issues. The overriding public interest in protecting the welfare of the children requires that the Courts be in a position to vary all Orders and Agreements made in relation to children where circumstances change.

91

Until February 1997 couples were unable to divorce in Ireland. February 1997 saw the coming into law of the Family Law (Divorce) Act, 1996.

Under the Family Law Act 1995 and the Family Law (Divorce) Act 1996, Courts have power to order trustees of a Pension Scheme to earmark or split pensions in favour of the non-member spouse.

A number of Family Law Acts refer specifically to mediation, The Judicial Separation and Family Law Reform Act, 1989, The Family Law Act, 1995, The Family Law (Divorce) Act, 1996, The Children Act, 1997. There is specific encouragement given to estranged spouses by the these Acts to resolve outstanding family difficulties by mediation in the first instance and by concluding a legal Separation Agreement. Under these Acts a Judge may adjourn proceedings in order for the parties to resolve the issues at mediation. Further, all communications made by the parties in mediation are inadmissible as evidence in any subsequent proceedings. In Ireland the High Court and Circuit Court have jurisdiction in relation to applications for judicial separation and divorce. Most cases are dealt with by the Circuit Court.

What some couples have done who have gone through FMS is to take their Mediated Agreement to the Circuit Court themselves. One of the spouses issues a Notice of Motion and serves it on the other which sets out that they intend applying to the Circuit Court on a specific date and time for the purposes of having the Mediated Agreement made a Rule of Court. Both spouses (Appellant and Respondent) attend before a judge who reads the Mediated Agreement to satisfy himself in relation to arrangements around the children and the financial provisions in the Agreement to see they are fair. The Agreement is then received into Court under the Family Law (Maintenance of Spouses and Children's) Act, 1976. The Agreement is then binding and enforceable.

The family outside marriage

The non-marital family is not recognised under Irish law as a legal unit nor does it possess the same legal rights and obligations as the family based on marriage. However financial arrangements around children can be made a Rule of Court.

Mediation and the Law Reform Commission (LRC)

The Law Reform Commission in its report on Family Courts 1996 stresses the importance of independent legal advice for parties involved in mediation so that parties are aware of their legal entitlements or expectations so that any waiver should be made knowingly and with full understanding of its legal consequences. The LRC's Report goes on to discuss the role of the Courts in reviewing unfair, improvident and unwise Agreements in relation to:-

a)   Agreements concerning custody of or access to children

        LRC confirm that there would be no practical advantage in extending the Courts power to review agreed arrangements and that as parents have rights to proceed under Section 11 of the Guardianship of Infants Act 1964 in circumstances where agreed arrangements appear to have failed that this gives them adequate safeguard.

b)   Agreements concerning financial and property matters

        The Report states "our Courts have very limited powers to vary the powers of an agreed settlement on financial and property matters. Many Agreements themselves provide for a periodic review, particularly in relation to the level of maintenance payments. In the absence of such terms there is no general power in the Courts to order variations even where he Agreement has been made a Rule of Court under Section 8 of the Family Law (Maintenance of Spouses and Childrens) Act, 1976. A Court may refuse an application to make an Agreement a Rule of Court under Section 8 of the 1976 Act on the basis that the absence of an appropriate Review Clause may render the Agreement unreasonable or unfair. By contrast, a spouse that believes that he or she has been short-changed by the Agreement may always apply for maintenance under the Family Law (Maintenance of Spouses and Children's) Act, 1976".

c)   Application to have an Agreement recorded or made a Rule of Court

        The LRC Report recommends that "In every case where an application is made to a Court to have an Agreement which affects the parties financial or property relationships, recorded or made a Rule of Court, there should be an obligation on the Court not to grant the application unless it is satisfied that the Agreement is a fair and reasonable one which in all the circumstances adequately protects the interests of the parties and of any dependant children.

        A similar rule already applies where application is made to have an Agreement made a Rule of Court under the Family Law (Maintenance of Spouses and Children) Act, 1976, and this has already prompted some judicial comment on the question of what constitutes a fair and reasonable agreement. It is reasonable to expect the judicial scrutiny of such agreements will be that much more intense where either party has not had the benefit of legal advice".

        The Recommendations of the LRC have not been implemented yet. In conclusion, in Ireland there is a procedure whereby a couple who have concluded a Mediated Agreement can apply themselves to Court to seek to have the Mediated Agreement made a Rule of Court which would then make it binding and legally enforceable. It is not usual for couples to proceed in this way at present.

NORWAY

From discussion with The Ministry of Children and Family Affairs in Norway and literature from them on the status of Agreement, I have been informed that since the 1st of January 1998 a couple who has gone through the mediation process may take their Mediated Agreement to the County Governor and ask the County Governor to make it enforceable. The new Marriage Act which came into force in January 1993 lays down that spouses with children under 16 years of age must attend mediation process before a separation or divorce case can be proceeded with. Every couple needs to obtain a Certificate of Mediation from a mediator. The Mediators Certificate states either that the couple has attended mediation or that the couple hasn't attended but the mediator does not report on the content of the mediation discussions. In Norway, before going to Court a couple must try mediation. If one party doesn't want to mediate the Mediator meets only with the party who agrees with mediation and signs the Mediation Certificate to this effect. It is compulsory to go to mediation but if one party refuses it does not preclude the party who wants to go to mediation from proceeding to Court.

In Norway, parenting is the only issue for mediation; however, ancillary issues do touch on parenting issues such as how the child will be maintained and that the parent who has parenting responsibility for the child will have a right of residence in the matrimonial home even if the title of the property is not in that parents name. When the couple brings their Mediated Agreement to the County Governor the County Governor checks to see that the Agreement is in the best interests of the child. The County Governor asks the parents whether they have told the child about the decision and how the child has responded to this. In Norway, when the child has reached the age of 12 he or she is allowed his or her opinion before decisions are made on personal matters on his or her behalf including which parent the child wishes to live with. Couples are offered four hours of mediation.

SCOTLAND

From information received from Family Mediation Scotland I have been informed that for the past two years a pilot programme of comprehensive mediation has been in place i.e. all issues arising in separation can be discussed and agreed upon. The Mediated Agreement is called a Memorandum of Understanding in Scotland. The couple take the Memorandum of Understanding to their solicitors who draws it up into a Minutive Agreement which is then presented to the Court as part of Divorce. The majority of couples separating in Scotland proceed to divorce.

The terms used in relation to children are "residence" and "contact". These terms have been used since legislation in 1996.

The Memorandum of Understanding has no legal standing by itself. In Scotland they decided after a lot of debate not to use the term "Mediated Agreement" as by using the word "agreement" it could be construed as a contract.

In Scotland couples separating or divorcing appear before the Sheriff Court.

Mediation is a voluntary process. Under Rules of Court the Sheriff can refer couples to mediation for an information session. If the parties decide not to proceed with mediation the mediator reports simply that they attended for the information session and that mediation did not proceed.

ENGLAND AND WALES

The status of a Mediated Agreement, from information received from Professor Janet Walker, Newcastle Centre of Family Studies, is that a Mediated Agreement is not legally binding in England and Wales. It is not unusual for couples to take an Agreement to their lawyers so that it can be incorporated into the Statement of Arrangements for Children and thereby endorsed by the Court. A couple cannot register their Agreement. It is not possible for a couple to make a Mediated Agreement enforceable. Divorce in England and Wales is dealt with by the County Court (Divorce Court) although Orders in relation to ancillary matters prior to Divorce proceedings can take place in the Magistrate's Court. If a couple include the substance of a Mediated Agreement within the Statement of Arrangements then the Judge will look at it because the Statement of Arrangements is considered by the Court. Mediation in England and Wales is seen as a voluntary process and on the whole the Courts do not get involved.

CONCLUSION

Information received from the countries mentioned above show that in order for Mediated Agreements to be legally binding and enforceable they must be endorsed by a court or judicial authority - This echoes the summary of the Preliminary Report of CJ-FA-GT2 on the Status of Mediated Agreements.

7.11   Summary:-

In order for mediated agreements to be legally binding and enforceable, in most States they must be endorsed by a court or judicial authority. In endorsing agreements courts must have regard to children's best interests and any legal rules regarding maintenance and soon.

REFERENCES

Family Mediation Service - Ground Rules of Mediation

Family Mediation Service - Standard Clauses in Note of Mediated Agreement

Family Mediation Service - Code of Ethics and Professional Conduct for Family Mediators

Mediators Institute Ireland - Policy Document No. 1 1995

Shatter's Family Law - 4th Edition, 1997, Publisher - Butterworths

Report of the Constitution Review Group 1994

Answer to Dail (Parliamentary) Question - 20th October 1993, Questions No. 192, 193, 194

Committee of Experts on Family Law (CJ-FA) - Working Party on Mediation and other Proce***sses to resolve Family Disputes (CJ-FA-GT2) - Preliminary Report on the Questionnaire on Family Mediation (CJ-FA-GT2 (97) 14).

PROMOTION OF AND ACCESS TO FAMILY MEDIATION

(INFORMATION PROGRAMMES OF ACCESS TO FAMILY MEDIATION AND NON-DISCRIMINATION)

Report presented by

Renate WINTER
Judge, at present consultant at the
Centre for International Crime Prevention,
United Nations,
Vienna, Austria

Summary

To address access to and promotion of family mediation, one must first establish who would provide access to mediation, and to what extent there is interest in doing so, so as to discover ways and means for promotion.

Mediation can be thought of as a supplementary working tool for the judge. In this case, it will be the government's duty to secure access and promotion.

Mediation can also be viewed as a real Alternative Dispute Resolution. The judiciary is not involved - or only to a limited extent - and as such it will be the role of the providers to make mediation publicly known and accepted.

Mediation may also be compulsory before a regular procedure can take place. In this third case, the government must find solutions not only for the access to and promotion of mediation, but also for the upcoming problems of discrimination and inequality before the law.

Austria took the first option and includes in its draft for a new divorce law voluntary mediation, executed through "co-mediation"-techniques by a psychologist and a lawyer.

Germany experiments with some kind of compulsory mediation in civil law matters, but has not yet decided upon how to deal legally with family matters. *Australia* opted for mediation through private services, leaving it to a great extent to the communities to look after access and promotion. On the other hand, "settlement weeks", a scheme to provide mediation in pending cases are supported by the courts.

Belgium is in a state of experimentation. A proper law does not exist, though mediation is done in the private sector on a profit-oriented basis.

Switzerland has dispositions in its laws to allow for voluntary mediation. Cantons have created mediation centres for the convenience of the public.

The United Kingdom begun its family mediation in the voluntary sector. The creation of semi-governmental institutions (or private institutions subsidized by the government) increases the possibilities for the public to have access.

In *Africa*, family mediation lies within the traditions of almost all countries. As there exists no regulation for this method of conflict resolution by traditional practices, a legal solution must be found to incorporate already existing good practices into the state law and to control them in the light of human rights.

Albania, which underwent considerable changes concerning state law in the course of its history, did not change its access to mediation to the same extent. A new law on mediation in civil, family and penal matters has been drafted to be submitted to the parliament.

To promote family mediation and to grant access to it for every advice-seeking person, a legal framework must be provided, mediation must be publicised to make it visible to and accepted by the public and the professionals, pilot projects and training possibilities must be established and fund-raising must occur. Governments as well as private providers have to be aware of the imminent danger of discrimination concerning topics as victims of violence in the family, gender-, money- and time problems, and mediation in transnational and intercultural cases.

Report

Recommendation No. R (98) 1, principle VI says to member states on family mediation that "States should promote the development of family mediation, in particular information programmes given to the public...."
If one wishes to address promotion of and the access to family mediation, one has first to find out what access looks like and who are the players involved. Only then it will be possible to decide what kind of promotion would be appropriate in a given situation.

Access to mediation

Access to mediation is maybe thought of in three ways, illustrating the importance a society gives to mediation (Riomet 1998).

a)   Mediation can be a supplementary working tool for the judge. As such, a judge maintains his or her central role and chooses a mediator in the same way he or she would choose an expert. In this case, information regarding the meaning, content, and availability of mediation, as well as a list of approved mediators, should be given to the judge. It would be the task of the government (i.e., the relevant ministries) to provide this information to the courts which deal with family matters (in many cases, family courts). The relevant ministries might include the ministries of justice, welfare, interior, youth and family, administration, information (or some combination thereof). The president of the courts involved would have to transmit such information to the judges concerned, as well as to the public (e.g., through publicity in corridors; leaflets in court waiting rooms).

b)   Mediation may also be viewed as a real alternative to classical legal procedures. In this case, a judge is not to be involved, if possible, or must act only as a notary or registrar. In this case, mediation serves as a form of real "Alternative Dispute Resolution". To promote information about mediation services, one must understand who is providing such services and who will be in charge of making such services known to the general public. This issue will be dealt with in speaking about the "players".

c)   Or, mediation may be made compulsory, as a necessity to undergo before a procedure can take place. In this case it is clear that it is the role of the government - through legislation - to provide information on and access to mediation. The government thus would have the following responsibilities:

- the creation of services;
- the maintenance of those services;
- the nomination of mediators;
- the provision of access to those services for any party concerned, even if a party could not otherwise afford to consult a mediator.

To make mediation compulsory and to provide access for all has several benefits: mediation relieves overburdened judges, who otherwise usually suffer under a steadily increasing workload; and mediation saves time in the administration of justice, and therefore saves money.

But the advantages of compulsory access to mediation for the public are not as straightforward. To illustrate, let us take a divorce case: Mrs. X wishes a divorce, Mr. X does not. If mediation is compulsory, Mr. X has now more possibilities than in a classical procedure to make the life of Mrs. X quite miserable (e.g., by not showing up for mediation under the pretext of being ill; by hindering the mediator in doing his/her job properly; by denying collaboration). If, as in this case, the legislation foresees an ending of mediation on the grounds of a lack of efficacy, compulsory mediation will quickly change into one more formal step to be added to the "normal" procedure.

In Germany, the legislature is now considering the introduction of a kind of mandatory mediation (bearing more of the characteristics of arbitration than of mediation, in my understanding) in some civil matters, so as to decrease both the workload of the judiciary and the often very long duration of procedure. Parties should be encouraged to accept mediation through the disposition that non-compliance will double the costs of procedure.

This means that a non-willing party not only has all the additional possibilities to be a hindrance, as mentioned in the example above, but has further ways and means if economically stronger. This could lead to the consequence of inequality before the law, which in no way could be the intention of mediation. Another case has been found in the new "Insolvenzordnung" (bill of insolvency) of Germany, in force from 1. January 1999. An agreement through extrajudiciary resolution between all creditors and the indebted persons is one of the mandatory prerequisites to a remission of debts (*Restschuldbefreiung*) in a private insolvency (*Privatkonkurs*).

If agreement cannot be reached, the mediator has to certify it, and only then can the procedure for the remission of debts be opened. Again it is easy to imagine that it would not be difficult for an economically advantaged creditor (e.g., a bank) to make mediation difficult, if not impossible, and therefore to undermine the position of the already weaker party, which again is in no way the intention of proper mediation.

The above-mentioned examples of compulsory mediation in Germany are not linked to family mediation, and they already appear not to be an only positive means of conflict resolution. Family mediation is a very sensitive technique in trying to solve very deep-reaching problems of never equally strong partners. If mediation is to become widely accepted, if it really should become an efficient tool for solving family problems more humanely than through court proceedings, equal chances of all parties involved have to be granted.

If mediation is compulsory, an ill-willing stronger party can victimise the weaker one without giving the mediator even a chance to intervene to make a procedure eventually possible. If mediation is voluntary (which is an inherent principle of any extrajudiciary conflict resolution), the weaker party can at least turn to the classical procedure without further obstacles.

In my understanding, compulsory mediation is a contradiction of itself. It is very dangerous for the principle of equality before the law, and it can easily lead to discrimination. Therefore, should a state envisage access to mediation via compulsion, legal guarantees have to be strong to prevent misuse.

A further thought should be given to the psychological side of compulsion: it does not invite conflict-driven parties to have faith in the conflict-resolution abilities of the mediator.

For all these reasons I believe that access to mediation on a free-will basis should be promoted to the greatest extend possible.

The Actors

Which institutions are able to provide access to mediation?

1.   The courts

There are first of all, the courts. They are involved, if a state opts for the possibilities a) and c) mentioned above.

THE CASE OF AUSTRIA (option a)

In the course of its deliberations concerning the "Report of Experts on the UN Convention on the Rights of the Child", the National Assembly called on the Federal Government (E 156 - NR/XVIII. GP, para. 8) to submit, on the basis of the results of scientific rescarch accompanying the pilot project "Family counselling at court, mediation and child guidance in divorce or separation cases", proposals for draft legislation and organisational measures which would lead divorce or separation seeking couples

1.   *to accept their own responsibility for resolving their partnership conflict, and*
2.   *to continue to exercise their parental responsibility in a form protecting the welfare of the child* (Filler 1998).

The pilot project "Family Mediation" started at two Austrian district courts in 1994 by decision of the Ministry of Justice (JMZ 1994). In 1996 and 1998, the Ministry decided to continue the project (Amtsblatt 1997, Amtsblatt 1998, respectively), setting up a collaboration between the Ministry of Justice, the Ministry of Environment, Youth and Family Affairs and the association "Co- Mediation".

The extent and guidelines of the project were accurately defined, and training for family-judges was provided, taking explicitly into consideration that there did not exist a legal basis for mediation in family-law proceedings, but that on the other hand the law did not exclude mediation. As a consequence, the participation of judges at the pilot project had to be absolutely volontary and there was no obligation of parties to undergo mediation.

Leaflets were prepared for couples interested in trying out this new method of conflict resolution. Judges involved in the pilot project were encouraged to recommend to parties to seek a solution for their problems through mediation rather than to choose the assistance of the courts.

On the basis of the initial positions and basic conditions briefly described above, the central task for implementing the pilot project family counselling at court, mediation, and supporting children when parents divorce or separate was as follows: in the case of matrimonial conflicts, the family court proceedings were to be linked with services which were to activate the personal potential for action of those involved (spouses, children) to enable them to participate in a controlled process of conflict resolution or conflict management on the basis of self-responsibility.

The services to be offered therefore had to be focused on three neuralgic areas:

1. *legal and psychological counselling prior to court proceedings (family counselling at court),*
2. *counselling and guidance regarding the "rules of the game" of the separation and the subsequent phase (mediation), and*
3. *the psychological support of children as the victims of a divorce or separation (child guidance).*

This theoretical profile was translated into a model design consisting of three project stages, mediation being the second part (Filler 1998).

Starting with a workshop meeting on 8 July 1994, a total of eight mediator teams, each consisting of one mediator from the legal and one from the psycho-social field, took up their work in accordance with the concept set up for the mediation element of the pilot project. Until the end of 1995 (in some cases until January 1996), five and three teams were operating in Vienna and Salzburg, respectively. The organisational course of the pilot project was based on a co-operation with the family judges at the Vienna/Floridsdorf and Salzburg district courts: The judges informed couples wishing to divorce or persons coming to them with guardianship questions about the existence of a mediation service. The decision as to which persons should be given a recommendation concerning mediation was taken at the judges' discretion. Altogether, a total of approximately ninety couples used the mediation service. While a smaller group discontinued the mediation process after the first session, the majority attended between two and eleven mediation sessions, each lasting from one to three hours each. In those cases where couples resorted to mediation, court proceedings were discontinued for a certain period (Pelikan et al. 1998).

Meanwhile family mediation as a service, promoted by the courts, is gradually expanding. There exists an association "Co-Mediation", where

102

about 25 mediator's teams located in different Austrian cities have joined together. The model of co-mediation as tried out in the pilot project has been adopted for the kind of family mediation that is promoted and recommended by the family (guardianship) judges. The association is responsible for the development and the control of professional standards of mediation. and thus also for the selection of its members.

Clients who have come to the courts for the initiative steps toward a divorce or for a rearrangement of custody or access regulations, and who wish to continue by way of mediation receive a list of the mediation teams of the association, cooperating with the courts. They contact a team of their choice and are supposed to pay the fee set up by the association. In case of low family income the couples making use of this kind of court-promoted mediation can ask for a reduced fee and the Ministry of Justice is prepared to supplement the regular mediation fee (Pelikan 1998).

To provide information about the costs from the very beginning, a chart was prepared in the leaflet and was distributed to couples seeking advice (cf. table).

Soviel kostet 1 Stunde Mediation für Sie :

Der auf den vollen Satz fehlende Betrag wird durch das BM für Umwelt, Jugend und Familie sowie das BM für Justiz subventioniert

Einkommen	Paare ohne Sorgepflicht	Paare mit einer Sorgepflicht	Eltern mit zwei oder mehr Sorgepflichtigen
bis 15.000,-	0,	0,-	0,-
von 15.000,- - 20.000,-	200,-	100,-	100,-
von 20.000,- - 25.000,-	800,-	400,-	200,-
von 25.000,- - 30.000,-	1.200,-	600,-	400,-
von 30.000,- - 35.000,-	2.000,-	1.200,-	800,-
von 35.000,- - 40.000,-	2.500,-	2.000,-	2.000,-
über 45.000,-	2.500,-	2.500,-	2.500,-

Unter Einkommen verstehen wir das durchschnittliche monatliche Netto-Familieneinkommen (ohne Familienbehilfe). Sondervereinbarungen sind bei getrennten Haushalten oder bei besonderen Härtefällen möglich. Die Sitzungen dauern zwischen 1 und 2 Stunden und werden nach der jeweiligen Dauer abgerechnet. Sollten Sie einen ermäßigten Betrag in Anspruch nehmen, ersuchen wir Sie, die erforderlichen Nachweise (z.. Gehaltzettel) zur ersten Sitzung mitzubringen.

The judge is to recommend, without sanction, to parties wanting to divorce that they should make use of the mediation facility, the basic principle of mediation being voluntary participation. Divorcing couples must never be pressed by the court, for example by the use of direct or indirect threats of legal or other drawbacks, to accept such an offer. The decision to try mediation in cases of divorce is exclusively taken in a deliberate agreement between the spouses willing to divorce (possibly represented by their lawyers), that is brought to the notice of the judge. The scope of application of mediation is not restricted to the divorce proceedings proper, but also includes such related cases as custody and access to the child. Even though the main purpose of mediation is to initiate and prepare for consensual divorce - frequently even before court proceedings are instituted - access to mediation will also be possible prior to a formally pending court proceeding.

During the course of mediation, it must be ensured that any material and formal statutory claims of the parties are fully protected, for example by the suspension of time limits. Conversely, court proceedings instituted at a previous stage may be continued at any time after a mediation process, for example, following the discontinuation of a failed mediation attempt. Along with the future perspective of a formal recognition of mediation, there will also be a restructuring of the role of the courts and, hence, of the family-law judges. The task of redesigning their functions will be part of the preparations for a reform of marriage and divorce law and, particularly, of the law on divorce procedure (Filler 1998).

After four years of preparation, the Committee on law reform in family matters at the Ministry of Justice includes voluntary family mediation in the draft for a revised divorce law (Diskussionsentwurf für EheSchrÄG, Art. 99, Mediation). To promote the idea of family mediation, the partners of the pilot project (i.e., the Ministry of Justice, the Ministry of Environment, Youth and Family Affairs) produced a video available for the interested public.

THE CASE OF GERMANY (option c)

Germany, as already mentioned above, gives priority to deliberations directed towards compulsory mediation for reasons concerning the administration of justice. However, many private organisations are providing family mediation sevices in the forefront of procedures on a voluntary and profit-oriented basis. At this point, the legislature does not seem to be interested in making mediation compulsory in the field of family law.

2.   Community Justice Programs and mediation through organisations, subsidized by governments and bar-associations, Legal Aid Offices

THE CASE OF AUSTRALIA (option b)

Community Justice Programs are based on governmental programmes, which give public access to mediation services and provide them cost-free. In most counties and territories of Australia, the development is directed towards extra-judicial conflict resolution. These programmes highlight community values, and the procedures of mediation are prescribed by law as well as training for and responsibilities of the mediators, who enjoy legal immunity.

Also, governments and the bar-associations subsidize private organisations such as UNIFAM or "Relationships Australia", which deal inter alia with family matters.

Legal Aid Offices exist in some of the countries. They have their own standards of professional behavior and provide continuous training for their mediators. In Queensland, for instance, "legal aid conferences" are compulsory (option c). If an agreement cannot be reached, it will be decided whether the parties will get financial support for a court proceeding.

"Settlement weeks" helped to make mediation well known in Australia (option a). During this period, parties involved in a pending court procedure have the possibility to find an agreement via mediation. "Settlement weeks" are provided each year by the Supreme Court and the District Courts of some Australian counties. One of the goals of this arrangement consists in promoting the acceptance of jurists for mediation. The courts support these programmes, and public funding is available (Spegel 1996).

3.   Private Mediation

THE CASE OF BELGIUM (option b)

The only legislative text referring to mediation is to be found in the Decret of 14.7.1994, in force since 1.1.1995, concerning the Centres of family-planning of the commission of the county "Brussels-capital". It states in its article 4, specifying the role of the centres, that: "...inter alia, the centres can develop specific activities in more specialised fields...., as family mediation...." (Volckrick 1998).

Family and divorce mediation is a relatively new field in Belgium, involving three professional sectors on a private basis:

- Private social welfare services, subsidized by the Flemish or French community (The Flemish Community is elaborating a specific Decret on family mediation);
- Counselors or psychologists, working on a totally private, profit oriented basis;
- Lawyers, who according to a new instruction of the National Bar Association can follow specialised training on divorce mediation (Aertsen 1998).

4.   Centres of Mediation

THE CASE OF SWITZERLAND (option a)

In Switzerland, family mediation is voluntary. The judge does not have the right to force spouses into mediation services (nor can he impose sanctions) if they dont want to undergo mediation. Among the biggest goals of the revision of the law of divorce are the depenalisation of divorce, the invitation to the spouses to settle divorces in an extrajudiciary manner, the protection of the interests of the children, and a just settlement of the financial consequences of the divorce (P. Meier 1997).

The number of practitioners offering their services in the light of this new development has considerably increased. Centres of mediation, "Les maisons de la Médiation" have been created in some of the cantons to inform the public, being a kind of platform of synergies between the different forms of mediation, coexisting in every such canton. The Centres enumerate all mediation forms and -types available in-house, thus facilitating the choice for advice-seeking parties (Knoepfler 1998).

5.   Private organisations

THE CASE OF ENGLAND (options a and b)

The introduction in 1979 of the first services of family mediation in Britain has been part of a development trend towards private ordering. This comparatively new approach to the management of disputes in the field of family breakdown is now an acknowledged part of legal policy and of the substantive law culminating in the Children Act of 1989.

The radical philosophy of the Children Act with its new principles of "parental responsibility" and "non-interventionism" embodies a view of the public interest that is defined, certainly in the private law, in terms of settlement through agreement.

More recently still, the Law Commission Divorce Reform Proposals (Law Com. 192, 1990) incorporate mediation as "an important element in developing a new and more constructive approach to the problems of marital breakdown and divorce." (para. 7.24) (Roberts 1992).

Thus, family mediation began in the UK in 1978 in the voluntary sector.

The concept derived most directly from a government report which studied the poverty of one parent families and recommended a family court with a "Conciliation Service" attached.

The first few Family Mediation Services, funded by Trusts and Charities, staffed by sessional mediators and governed by trustees, publicised themselves locally via the local press and the network of relevant professionals, some of whom comprised the trustees (judges, family lawyers, socia1 workers, probation officers etc). In the courts, judges and court welfare officers experimented with "In Court Conciliation", giving the option to parents attending court. The practice spread throughout the 1980's, gaining in professionalism and almost entirely provided by the voluntary sector. Mediation focussed at this stage solely on arrangements for children. Led by the national body now called "National Family Mediation", national publicity and political interest was sought and at times attracted, leading to a major research being commissioned by the government, which received significant press attention when published in 1989. This studied both "In-court" conciliation, provided by the statutory court welfare service and "Out-of-court" mediation, provided by NFM's 40 or so local Services.

In 1989, the Family Mediators Association formed in the private sector provided the mediation of finance and property as well as children issues. It

106

also attracted some national publicity. An Interdisciplinary Forum formed to foster dialogue about family proceedings and mediation was a catalyst for this development, which served to further professional interest in the concept and practice. The new Children Act, 1989, though expressing some of the key ideas of the 1980's, in which mediators played an influential part, did not specifically include or mention mediation in its provisions. In Scotland and Northern Ireland, some public funding was made available for family mediation in the voluntary sector; similar Services in England and Wales did not receive any public funding.

In 1992, the Joseph Rowntree Foundation published research commissioned by NFM into its own practice of "All Issues Mediation" (finance and property as well as children issues). This attracted media interest. The government also became interested as it was in the process of devising a new divorce law, based on proposals from the Law Commission, which had included mediation in its recommended provisions. In 1992/3 a great deal of media interest was generated by the publishing of the Divorce Law Green Paper entitled "Looking to the Future: mediation and the ground for divorce".

The ensuing Familiy Law Bill was unexpectedly affected by a surge of political resistance to certain provisions in a Domestic Violence Bill which became linked to it.

It was overtaken by a surge of media interest engulfing the management of divorce with a wave of concern about marriage and "family values". The Family Law Bill, creating a central role for mediation, produced therefore a great deal of political, professional and media interest in mediation. The actual take-up of Mediation, however, did not advance greatly during this period, as the existing law gave it no place and no funding. Its promotion to prospective clients remained the sole responsibility of the mediators in the voluntary and private sectors. The Family Law Act contains several sections which give opportunities for take-up of mediation. They are:

1. *Compulsory provision of information to those intending to initiate divorce proceedings. This information includes information about mediation.*

2. *Requirement for solicitors to inform clients about the availability of mediation.*

3. *Requirement for those seeking legal aid for legal representation first to attend a meeting with a mediator to learn about mediation and to consider its suitability.*

4. *A power for the courts to order a meeting with a mediator to consider mediation.*

5. *Public funding for mediation for those eligible for legal aid.*

These opportunities stop short of making mediation compulsory but, when implemented, are likely to give many, perhaps most, people an opportunity to understand and consider mediation. The Information Meetings, now being piloted, include in the group sessions a video of mediation. The legal aid "meetings with a mediator" is now also being piloted, bringing people face to face with a mediator to learn about mediation. Public funding for mediation is proceeding via franchises, with some publicity given by the Legal Aid Board locally as well, as local franchised suppliers making the most of the granting of their pilot franchise to publicise their services. Once the mediation franchise pilot has progressed far enough both in availability and in quality assurance, then the Legal Aid Board say they will give mediation greater national publicity. The goal of the government, expressed through the Legal Aid Board, is to provide a range of suppliers - in the private and voluntary (not-for-profit) sectors. How far they are seeking to ensure provision at all major centres of population is not yet clear, although the mediation bodies are working to that end themselves when resources allow.

The government is protected against not having the meeting with a mediator available by new regulations which state that the requirement is only enforceable where a mediator is available within 14 days (Fisher 1998).

6.   The tribal mediation

THE CASE OF AFRICA (option b)

Africa, the plagued continent, will stand in this exposé as an example for almost every developing country. In these countries, the rule of law is very often not respected, the judiciary is usually not in good shape, sometimes more or less non-existing. But concerning mediation, there is not really very much to learn for let us say the equivalent of a justice of peace, for instance in a Tuareg tribe in Niger, for a chief of a Berber settlement in Morocco or for a wizard in a Bushman's tribe in South-Africa. Many good ideas and practices can be found and conflict resolution in an extrajudiciary way is a long standing tradition, still in use today, due very often to the lack of judges and the administration of justice. A Tuareg or Berber chief would act as mediator in a family conflict, going from one party to the other, until the conflict is settled. In a South-African tribe, the chief, the priest, the wizard, the doctor, (sometimes any other respected person) will convoke the members of both (or all) families involved and the meeting will end only after the conflict has been solved. To grant access to or to promote mediation is therefore not a problem in these types of countries. The problem is that judges can accept mediation only within the law. This means, that one has to find possibilities for inserting the already practiced mediation in the legislative framework to make it a legal tool (South-Africa is currently drafting such a new law). This legislative framework has to be in accordance with the international instruments, as for instance the European Convention on Human Rights or the UN-Convention of the rights of the child. This accordance is very important, as traditional ways of conflict resolution can be very cruel in comparison to modern standards on Human Rights.

7.   From the Canun towards a modern legislation

THE CASE OF ALBANIA (option a)

Albania is in many ways (not in all) an example for the development of post- communist countries. The system of mediation can be found in the old Canun, the regulatory system of the Albanian clans, dating back to the middle ages. It treats inter alia family matters up to blood-feud. Its most important propositions for solving even serious conflicts would be called today mediation, provided by a person respected for his/her virtues by both groups involved (Elezi 1998).

In the socialist system, a kind of extrajudiciary conflict-resolution was provided, especially when young persons were involved. The managers of such a "mediation" were only persons trustworthy to the political party, not to the same extent to the family members involved.

It is therefore sometimes a problem during discussions or workshops in preparation of new laws or methods to explain to judges or legislators in post-communist countries the real meaning of mediation. Thus the reaction is very often treacherouly positive, due to a mixing up of notions. It is only in post-communist countries such as Albania, where mediation traditions date back to times far before the socialist systems, that this danger is not so great.

The Albanian family is undergoing important changes in its structure, economic factors, births, marriages, divorces, life-style, and the fulfilment of its functions have marked new tendencies.

Although to a lesser extent than in countries such as Russia, the Czech Republic, or Estonia, divorce is a disturbing social problem with grave consequences for poor Albanian families. The number of children caught in divorces is two times bigger than in 1985. The increase of divorces, the poverty of a great number of Albanian families, the emigration of at least one parent, families with parents having serious problems, have all caused a great risk for the education and the wellbeing of children. As long as there are no solutions to those problems mentioned above, the workload of the already overburdened Albanian courts will increase significantly. The tendencies concerning the increase of family problems and the increase in the number of children coming to court is influenced by the lack of quick and timely interference of the society (Hysi 1998).

Therefore, to overcome the deficencies in the administration of justice, the Albanian legislator drafted a law "on mediation towards reconciliatory resolution of disputes of the republic of Albania". This law has been already commented on in 1998 by experts of the Council of Europe (Riomet, Christie, Brydensholt) and is ready to be discussed in parliament.

Conclusions

What are now the possibilities to promote family mediation and to grant access to it for anyone seeking help and advice ?

- The creation of a legal framework, which provides for the possibilities of mediation (the United Nations drafted a model-law for countries, interested in adapting their laws in this regard).

- Publicity via the media, via the actors concerned, (e.g., Presidents of courts, relevant NGOs, private associations through movies, videos, leaflets, posters etc).

- Pilot projects to find the best solutions for the respective countries.

- Publications of researchers in the field for the use of practitioners.

- Seminars and training workshops run on a bilateral or international basis for the judiciary involved, as well as for other interested professions (e.g., doctors, lawyers, sociologists, psychologists).

- Creation of Centers for Mediation, Legal Aid Offices, Maisons de Justice, legal clinics, etc.

- Establishment of bibliographies available for practitioners and researchers.

- Fund-raising activities in illustrating the advantages of the mediation to give mediation a high profile.

THE DANGER OF DISCRIMINATION

Recommendation 1074(1988) of the Parliamentary Assembly of the Council of Europe on family policy articulates in its point 17., A. v. as follows:

"To revise criminal and civil legislation concerning violence in the family, and to encourage psychological and other measures of assistance to the victims and perpetrators of violence, without prejudice to the legal procedures concerning the latter."

This recommandation leads to the question of whether or not mediation services will make the already stronger party in a conflict even more strong.

A)   Violence in the family

In Austria, a pilot project deals with cases of violence in the family. Women's associations are strongly opposing this undertaking and point out that a battered woman is in no way a match for the perpetrator within the family. Furthermore, they stress the fact that the only valuable reaction to violence against spouses and children must be a criminal case to make society understand that violence in the family will no longer be tolerated.

The advocates for mediation in these cases argue that a long-lasting solution can never be found through penal court proceedings.

Exactly the same discussion goes on in the United States, where women's associations already have succeded in some counties to exclude cases of family violence from mediation.

The position of the Battered Women's Coalition has been that mediation is not appropriate for any woman who does not have power and bargaining skills that equal those of her husband. A recent report on the subject is that of the Toronto Forum on Woman Abuse and Mediation, which addresses four major areas of concern and makes the following recommendations:

1. Training and education of family mediators on woman abuse;
2. Pre-mediation screening, if the case is suitable for mediation;
3. Safety and specialised mediation for the protection of abused persons;
4. Alternatives to mediation, in case mediation is not possible (Mc Knight).

B)   Gender

In some societies, being a woman requires that one has to listen rather than to speak and to stand for one's rights. Therefore, many women are not accustomed to argue for their rights and tend to accept compromises to their detriment. Psychologists and psychiatrists point out that in these cases women would need therapy before being able to participate in a mediation programme.

C)   Money

If mediation services are not provided free of charge, or, as again shown by the Austrian model, if they will not be subsidized by justice or welfare, the access of the poorer segment of the population will not be granted.

D)   Time

A lack of time arises in connection with gender: if one of the spouses (usually the woman) must look after the children without any assistance - and if this person has to go to work as well - there will be no time remaining for time-consuming programmes such as mediation .

E)   Legislation's responsibility

If mediation is compulsory as mentioned above, the non-willing party can prohibit the access of the other to the regular court proceedings. If mediation is voluntary, on the other hand, the non-willing partner can prohibit the access of the other to mediation. In both cases regulations have to be installed to prevent discrimination against the willing party.

F)   Transnational and international mediation

In a time in which marriages cross the borders of states, cultures and religions ever more frequently, Centres should be established where mediation may take place, even if one of the parties would be denied access according to his or her own cultural background. Such Centres exist for instance in Switzerland for violence and conflict situations of intercultural origin for foreigners, immigrants and individuals living in "mixed" (e.g., multinational) families. In drafting laws or dispositions on mediation, legislators must not forget to include regulations for alternative conflict resolution regarding such "mixed" families.

References

Aertsen I. 1998, Université Catholique de Louvain, Belgium,
private communication
Elezi I. 1998, Faculty of Law, Univ. of Tirana, Albania, expert statement
Filler E. 1998,
in Family Counselling at Court, Mediation, Child Guidance in Divorce Cases,
Austrian Federal Ministry of Environment, Youth and Family Affairs,
Verlag Österreich, Wien 1998, pp. 18, 77, 83
Fisher T. 1998, UK College of Family Mediators, private communication
Hysi V. 1998, Faculty of Law, Univ. of Tirana, Albania, expert statement
Knoepfler J., "Médiation et fédéralisme: le défi suisse romand", in "Médiation",
La Lettre de la Médiation en langue française, direction: J.-P. Bonafé-Schmitt,
n° 31 (décembre 1998)
McKnight M. 1998, Director of Family Mediation Services in Minneapolis,
USA, private communication
Meier P., 1997, in Repères/Revue Romande d'Information Sociale 17/97, p. 9
Pelikan C. et al. 1998,
In Family Counselling at Court, Mediation, Child Guidance in Divorce Cases,
Austrian Federal Ministry of Environment, Youth and Family Affairs,
Verlag Österreich, Wien 1998, p. 40
Riomet N. 1998, in document DEMO-Exp (98) 1, Council of Europe,
Jan. 8 1998
Roberts M. 1992, in Journ. Soc. Welfare and Family Law, Sept. 1992, p. 372
Spegel N. 1996, in Betrifft JUSTIZ 48, Dec. 1996, p. 387
Volckrick E. 1998, Université Catholique de Louvain, Belgium,
private communication.

GENERAL REPORT

presented by

Igor DZIALUK
Deputy Director of Judicial Assistance and European Law
Ministry of Justice
Warsaw, Poland

For many years now the feeling of crisis for families in Europe coincides with constant information on the crisis in the justice systems. This is probably why family mediation attracts so much attention, offering, at first sight, a possible solution to both of them.

Mediation as a method of alternative (should this expression be changed to "appropriate" ?) dispute resolution attracts attention world-wide. A number of countries has recently introduced, or intends to introduce it in different fields of public life. A question arises: is it possible to treat all those different forms of mediation as one phenomenon, or is mediation in family matters a specific type? A comparison of different definitions shows apparently numerous common features of mediation (e.g. the definition used by national Family Mediation as quoted by Susan Stewart, and the one of Tony Marshall in relation to victim-offender mediation). Also the three distinguishing factors of divorce mediation contained in Janet Walkers' contribution to "Restorative Justice on Trial", 1992, show common features: - a dispute resolution mechanism alternative to legal procedures, - control of the parties to the disputes over the decision making, - informality. Principles of voluntary involvement and of confidentiality have been also added.

If so, one could ask if family mediation differs significantly enough from other types of mediation to justify the particular interest manifested in the present Conference ? In other words, is it only the substantial scope of family mediation that makes it special ?

One of possible criteria discussed is the belief that family mediation deals with family (social) problems rather than with legal ones. It is true and false at the same time. Family mediation operates within the legal framework, deals with problems obviously linked with legal issues: how one can distinguish what is "legal" and what is not. It may happen, and it often happens, that the outcome of mediation creates a new legal situation for the parties.

Another feature that surely distinguishes mediation in family matters is its orientation towards the future. Parties to the mediation will, and certainly shall maintain contacts with each other, either living under one roof, or getting in touch over a number of issues that are anchored in their past spent together.

Recommendation No. R (98)1 displays several special characteristics of family matters, that need to be taken into account while addressing mediation in those issues.

Janet Walker emphasised on emotional and personal relationships that often go together with family disputes; and their impact on other family members, notably children; but other family members should not be neglected. She also pointed out that legal process with all its formalities may undermine these fragile relationships. Although the ultimate goal of justice is to settle the conflict rather than simply to "render a judgment", the system often fails to do that (for a number of different reasons). Family mediation is therefore designed to promote communication and reduce conflict between prospective actors in judicial proceedings.

The survey done by the Council of Europe before the Recommendation has been passed and the discussion of this forum shows that there still is some confusion in member States as to the aims and methods of mediation and those of conciliation, family counselling, therapy, etc. The question may be asked, however, if it is at all possible to make a clear distinction here, and to introduce any of those "pure and simple" models in life. Theoretic models have already been created some years ago; now it is time to see how they can operate in reality. If the model does not work - *tant pis* for the model [never mind the model].

The map of mediation in Europe remains diversified. In some countries mediation in family matters precedes adjudication, in others it remains totally independent from or replaces judicial proceedings. The cases may be selected for mediation either by the judiciary or by the parties themselves. The scope of mediation is different. The process is being led by state agencies or by associations and even private persons. The qualifications of mediators, training, costs of mediation etc. remain differentiated. It has been pointed out also that the traditions of each country should not be neglected.

Diversity remains therefore another key word for the understanding of the Recommendation. It does not aim at "harmonisation" of practices throughout Europe in the 40 member States. It offers, however, a set of common principles.

Once diversity is accepted, it is hard to find an "European" common "denominator". The elaboration of common European standards of action in mediation, rendering "good services" so to speak is however possible. This may be the role of the Council of Europe, the only truly pan-European organisation whose principal interests deal with the constitution of legal systems. Close co-operation with NGOs and governmental organisations - a mosaic of them introduced themselves at the Conference - should be secured in order to provide for a useful result.

Parties are able to negotiate their own agreed joint decisions with the help of an impartial mediator who has no authority to impose a settlement. A mandate for the mediator comes from the parties, who should be more willing to respect their own common decision eventually taken at the end of the day, rather than that "imposed" by the court.

Mediation may be organised in a number of ways, although the process is broadly similar, with mediators subscribing to a set of common principles and recognising the importance of training and the maintenance of quality standards. As co-operation across States increases, there is likely to be a growing demand for mediation in family matters which crosses national boundaries. Family mediation upholds the importance of family life to children and the need for social support for parents who separate and divorce. Research has shown that mediation is not appropriate for all families, but for those who do mediate successfully, the quality of life can be much improved.

Other principles set out in the Recommendation are based mainly on the notions of impartiality and neutrality, said Nathalie Riomet. The discussion has shown that although, in general, there is no problem with the acceptance of these two principles, their concrete understanding may differ.

Impartiality applies to mediators themselves and refers to their attitude towards the parties in the mediation.

While the neutrality requirement is more associated with the process itself, it became clear that the notion refers rather to the personal qualities of a mediator: different alternative proposals have been launched, all being associated rather with "multipartiality".

Again, the ideal model is practically non existent. "Perfect neutrality" might be even detrimental to the aims of mediation - the presumption of equality of the parties in family mediation is not always true. Moreover, it shall be noted that the protection of child's interest and welfare remains one of the major objectives of the process of mediation, and in consequence, the mediator must in certain cases put aside his "neutrality".

In this context, the European Convention on the Exercise of Children's Rights shall be mentioned, which shall be seen as yet another set of principles applicable to the mediation procedures as well. Member States should be encouraged to sign and ratify this instrument.

Selection proceedings, training and verification of qualifications of mediators are indispensable for family mediation to serve its aims.

In different countries the process of selection and training vary considerably. Only a few countries have established permanent training systems for mediators.

According to Sirpa Taskinen, people who need training in mediation can be divided into three categories: professionals who may encounter underlying marital stress in the course of their jobs, social workers and family doctors who have a wide range of duties and who are expected to come across of different problems of the families, and finally "a relatively new group of professionals in agencies, which specialise in mediation".

This part of the discussion dealt with requirements to be met by the third group rather than concentrating on different patterns of selection and training, that vary so much from country to country. A set of principles might be possibly elaborated under the aegis of the Council of Europe.

The different roles played by different interested groups would furthermore call for different training. The training programmes vary from one week up to two years. A new era is beginning in 1998, as the Institut universitaire Kurt Bösch (Sion, Valais) is to arrange a post-graduate training qualification in mediation. There are several partner universities collaborating in the programme. A course called "European Master in Mediation" will be arranged from November 1998 to December 2000.

High expectations placed with the mediators inevitably raise the question of professionalisation. There was almost unanimous support to the need for training offered to mediators. Verification and accreditation seem to be the next logical step forward, although it has not been yet introduced in most of the countries. Possible future development might be the acceptance of a new profession. The problem is not very recent; indeed, it has been already raised, for example, by Jean-Pierre Bonafé-Schmitt some years ago. The issue remains controversial, and it would be unrealistic to expect this Conference to give concrete solutions. What is probably more important is to have competent mediators.

The relationship between family mediation and legal proceedings was addressed by Antonio Farinha. The analysis of the relationship between family mediation and legal proceedings leads to the relationship between family mediation and justice, and in particular to legitimate expectations to protect family life, and to the effectiveness of judicial solutions to family problems.

The discussion has shown that there should be neither the spirit of competition nor incorporation in the relations of the two proceedings. The cases referred to mediation are normally those that might (and sometimes actually will) end up before the court. In this sense mediation should be seen as an alternative method of dispute resolution, but not in competition to judicial proceedings. At the Conference one had the impression that (at least verbally) representatives of judiciary were more open to this idea, while mediators emphasised their numerous failures to convince judges what mediation actually was.

Family mediation shows considerable advantages vis a vis judicial proceedings, preventing the aggravation of conflict and permitting regulation of family conflicts in consensual way. It should therefore be underlined that the two different types of procedure shall be seen as complementary to each other rather than concurring. The judge is definitely not the person best suited to enter into mediation within the judicial proceedings- neither is the court room the best place to do it.

The above conclusion should not, however, prevent entrusting judges to refer cases for mediation.

It is most often the case that the agreement achieved needs to be verified and approved by a judge in order to be enforceable. It should be, however, borne in mind, that the power of a mediated agreement lies in the readiness of the parties to enter mediation, and to follow voluntarily what has been finally mutually accepted. Mediation in any way may not prevent the parties to refer the case to the judiciary, if such a need arises, although a judge should, whenever appropriate, take the mediated agreement into consideration. It is important to assure the correct articulation and integration of the judiciary and non-judiciary interventions. The discussion shows that this problem has been slightly neglected in the past.

The key factor to understand the relations between mediation and justice is the simple fact that the objective of family mediation - the establishment of an agreement and the adoption of a functional communication for the future - remains also one of the principal goals of justice.

The Recommendation obliges the States to facilitate the approval of mediated agreements by a judicial authority or other competent authority where parties request it and provide mechanisms for enforcement of such approved agreements according to national law. It is not clear if this provision has been duly taken into account.

This tackles again the very basic relation between the mediation (as a service rendered) and standard ("regular") judicial procedure. It should be acknowledged again in this context that mediation should not be contradictory to judicial proceedings.

The problem of promotion of and access to family mediation was addressed by Renate Winter. Her point that the number of cases referred to mediation (either by the judiciary or private persons) significantly varies according to public awareness of its accessibility must be shared. Surveys have shown that the public in general knows little about mediation, and it may be assumed that even members of judiciary are not necessarily among those best informed.

According to the speaker, if mediation is thought of as a supplementary working tool for the judge, then it is primarily the government's duty to secure access and promotion. Otherwise (when mediation is to be viewed as a real alternative dispute resolution), it should be up to the providers to make mediation publicly known and accepted. This distinction seems to be fair and realistic. It should be noted, however, that the Recommendation does not distinguish this difference, and requires the State to promote mediation in either form.

Although one of the basic principles of mediation is that of voluntary participation, the Recommendation acknowledges that it is not contrary to its spirit to make it compulsory for the parties to meet with a mediator, who should provide the parties with full information on the basics of mediation, and its possible consequences including costs.

While discussing the access to family mediation, particular attention should be paid to the issue of providing equal access to mediation in certain regions, usually those that are underdeveloped. Another problem may be posed concerning access to mediation by those who are not in the position to afford it - here, application of legal aid schemes may be of assistance.

International aspects of family mediation seem yet to stay in the shadow, as the panel discussion has shown, although impressing experience was presented. Mediation might be seen as a useful tool to render solutions in "transfrontier" family disputes, where the now existing instruments and procedures are very often accused of being too formalised and non efficient. Indeed, practice shows that the co-operation of the parties, usually the abductive parent (who therefore is placed in an irregular position) is required to deal with the case. Judicial procedure - formalised and time-consuming - seems to be the least appropriate way of deciding with the problem. Cases under the Hague Child Abduction Convention and the Luxemburg Custody Convention were mentioned. However, one need to be aware of the fact that other problems and drawbacks related to "transfrontier" cases may also hamper mediation - a necessity to travel in order to participate in the meetings, problems of communication related to language skills, possible irregular status of one of the parties etc. One needs to be cautious that mediation is not used as a dilatory tactic here.

Recommendation No. R 98(1) is important not only because it encourages member States to introduce, promote and strengthen family mediation as an appropriate process for resolution of family disputes of different types. It is also an act – the first of its kind - that acknowledges the importance of family mediation for the communities of Europe in the changing social context. The Recommendation may not be therefore perceived as a final and completed legal instrument. It sketches merely the background for the independent development of mediation. Possible follow-up to the Conference was presented by Margaret Killerby, who also commented on the work carried out in different committees within the Council of Europe. It should be made clear that the Recommendation should not end up in the archives as a document whose only aim was to be adopted. In fact, the interest raised at the Conference proves that the Recommendation has all the chances of remaining a living instrument. The European Committee on Judicial Co-operation of the Council of Europe, therefore, shall invite member States to report on the implementation of its provisions, even if only a relatively short time has elapsed since it was passed by the Committee of Ministers.

The present Conference brought together two groups of people who are the most interested in shaping mediation: practitioners and jurists who have already made their effort to give a European legal framework to mediation procedures. The model is not petrified, and will develop in the near future. The interrelation between those two groups is a must: mediators need to act within the limits set up by the law, but on the other hand, policy makers and law drafters require input from practitioners.

CONCLUSIONS OF THE CONFERENCE

The Conference proposed:

"I. institutions: Together with family mediation organisations and other bodies or

    a.   to co-operate in the provision of technical assistance to States wishing to set-up family mediation including the setting-up of Pilot Projects;

    b.   to assist in the development of transfrontier family mediation especially in order to help children, whose parents live in different States, to remain in contact with both parents and to minimise the risk of child abduction;

    c.   to encourage all bodies and persons concerned (including judges and lawyers) to respond positively to family mediation and to promote its development;

    d.   to promote the training and accreditation or recognition of family mediators, in particular special training for international mediators, and to promote the role of family mediation associations.

II.   to continue the work in the field of family law and, where necessary, to assist States to adopt rules which help to avoid or reduce family disputes.

III.   to publish the Proceedings of the Conference together with the Recommendation on family mediation.

IV.   to promote the mediation process in order to resolve problems concerning not only the family but also other areas involving two or more parties".

CLOSING SPEECH BY

the Right Honourable the Lord IRVINE OF LAIRG,
Lord Chancellor of Great Britain

Ladies and gentlemen,

It gives me great pleasure to be here today.

I would like to begin by thanking you for inviting me to give the closing address for this historic Conference on Family Law, the first Conference organised by the Council of Europe on the topic of family mediation. I am very pleased to see that so many delegates from so many countries have joined in your discussions. It is extremely encouraging to see this wide appreciation of the potential of mediation in family cases.

Let me also congratulate the Council of Europe for organising this Conference and, more generally, for their promotion of mediation. The Committee of Ministers has already made a Recommendation to members States on family mediation. We are dilighted to say that the United Kingdom had the opportunity to participate fully in its drafting. Like many other nations represented at this Conference, we are enthusiastic to promote the use of mediation in family disputes, particularly to resolve conflicts over property; money and children between couples who have decided to divorce or separate. Our strong belief is that the effective use of mediation can reduce bitterness and acrimony. That is good for the individuals who are divorcing ; good for their children ; and good for our wider society and for the taxpayer funding those public services which have to pick up the pieces.

I imagine that, by now, I must be preaching to the converted. We will all agree that mediation has many advantages over litigation as a means of resolving disputes. First mediation reduces conflict. Parties are given the opportunity to hear each other's point of view face to face. They are able to negotiate a resolution for their problems themselves with the help of a mediator. As a result, they are better able to understand each other and to appreciate each other's opinions.

And simple agreement is not the end of the story. The beneficial effects of mediation are felt long after the mediation sessions have been finished. When mediation is successful, it is essentially a forward-looking process. It looks beyond the immediate point of contention to the development of an improved dialogue which will enable future questions, future differences to be resolved. This forward-looking caracteristic is what makes mediation so attractive.

Secondly, mediation is more constructive than adversarial court proceedings. Litigation usually serves only to reinforce already entrenched positions. In particular, litigation does not have the same forward-looking caracteristic – it deals with the issues presented to the court, that is, the issues currently in dispute. It rarely offers an easy means of solving future problems – at least not without a great deal of expenditure and, usually, heartache. Court proceedings can have the effect of damaging the relationship between the parties further. Both can experience resentment and triumph. Where there is everything to play for, family cases become a battleground – a war in which there are no winners, only losers. Mediation challenges entrenched positions and enables people to find a way forward which is acceptable to them, a way which enables both sides to be winners.

Thirdly, parties are more likely to adhere to agreements they have made themselves rather than orders that have been imposed from outside. The agreements reached in mediation have a rational basis. They are the result of constructive negotiations between those concerned. People are able to see or imagine that scoring points and settlings rounds will not be helpful for the future and that, in order to ensure the best arrangements for their own future, and that of their children, it is better to discuss problems and reach a sensible agreement which both parties regard as acceptable. This agreement will be their agreement. Both parties will feel more committed to keeping their part of the bargain.

Finally, by reducing conflict, mediation helps reduce the financial costs of resolving disputes. It is in everyone's interest to reduce the cost of using the family justice system to save or to end marriages. The more acriminious the parting, the more costly the proceedings. The more the lawyers are involved, the more they are paid, and the smaller the pot of money to be divided between the divorcing couple. Mediation will help reduce cost and will allow for a more co-operative approach to resolving disputes.

As you have heard over the past two days, each country is feeling its way towards the best – the most effective – means of using mediation. There is no suggestion that one model will fit all nor that one country's solution offers all the answers.

In England and Wales, we have been working for many years towards reducing the acrimony of divorce by the greater use of mediation. We are note there yet, though we are a long way down the road.

Countries which are keen to follow the mediation route will face many difficulties, many pitfalls. We in Britain have also faced them and believe we have found solutions which fit our circumstances. These solutions are, at least in part, embodied in the Family Law Act 1996.

This Act has two critical purposes.

First, to support the institution of marriage. Support for marriage and for the family is at the heart of the Government's strategy for modernising Britain. Marriage is one tried and tested means of delivering the stability children need and crave. The Government believes that, if couples choose to marry in order to offer their children stability and security, then we should offer them our support. For this reason one of the key objectives of the Family Law Act is to provide for couples contemplating divorce to be encouraged to consider whether their marriage really is over and to consider whether marriage counselling might be helpful, before they take the final step to divorce.

The British Government, however, accepts that in many cases it will not be possible to repair broken marriages. So the second objective underlying the Family Law Act is that, where all attempts to save a marriage have failed and the marriage has broken down irretrievably, it should be brought to an end with the minimum distress to the parties and any children affected ; and with any questions dealt with in a manner designed to promote as good a continuing relationship between the parties and any children affected as is possible in the circumstances.

We also believe that mediation is a powerful means of achieving this second policy objective. So mediation is central to the thinking behind the divorce reforms in the Family Law Act. The Government is determined that as many people as possible know what medition offers and are given the opportunity to benefit.

It is vital to minimise acrimony and emotional distress in family cases because people will often need to have a continuing relationship with one another beyond their lives living together. Why ? Because they have continuing responsibilities for their children. Mediation strikes the balance between achieving a satisfactory outcome for today and preserving as reasonable a relationship between the parties as the circumstances permit for the benefit of tomorrow.

Let me say a little more about how we expect mediation to work in practice. Following implementation of Part II of the Family Law Act in late 1999 or early 2000, parties wishing to apply for divorce or separation will be required to attend an information meeting. At this meeting the question of support for marriage will be addressed, together with the possibility of state-funded marriage counselling in appropriate circumstances. However, information will also be given about a number of other issues as required by the Act, including the resolution of disputes and the facilities offered by mediation. The information meeting will draw to people's attention that mediation can be a viable alternative to litigation and to arms-length negotiations through solicitors. We expect this to encourage mediation as an integral part of the divorce process.

Under the terms of Part III of the Act, the Government is now making state-funded mediation available for family proceedings through the agency of the Legal Aid Board, including both proceedings for divorce and separation and also proceedings taken by unmarried parents under the Children Act of 1989.

The Legal Aid Board began offering contracts to mediations suppliers for the supply of state-funded mediation in 1997, initially in 12 areas. By this means state-funded mediation is being made widely available. In 1998 further contracts will be offered extending the provision to further areas. It is planned to extend the provision of publicly-funded mediation to all areas of England and Wales by the year 2000. At the end of the first contracts, further contracts will be granted in the areas concerned. States-funded mediation is therefore already a reality in England and Wales and will remain so in the future.

The contracts have been awarded to several different types of family mediation agencies : to firms of solicitors, to not-for-profit mediation services and also to commercial mediation services. In the United Kingdom, family mediators deal exclusively with family proceedings, and do not deal with other types of mediation. Some services, particularly the not-for-profit mediation services, deal only with disputes over children. However, services are increasingly adapting themselves to deal with "all issues" mediation and will therefore also address disputes over property and finance.

Meeting the requirements of the franchising process presents a significant challenge to all mediation agencies seeking to participate in the family mediation project. The management and administrative requirements, not least the need to screen clients for domestic violence, represent a fairly dramatic cultural change for many agencies. It is for this reason that additional financial and practical assistance is required for the development of mediation services.

As part of the project to provide publicly-funded mediation, funding has therefore been given to the main Mediation agencies to help train and accredit mediators and to manage mediation services. Assistance is also being provided for the development of professional management skills in mediation services to enable the agencies to provide quality-assured mediation. The UK College of Family Mediators, which was formed in 1996 to help provide a unified professional identity for family mediators has been given funding to allow to it develop a Code of Practice and common professional standards for family mediators ; a disciplinary Code ; and a Complaints Procedure. The UK College has also published a Directory and Handbook, which includes details of all family mediation services and all individual family mediators who are members of the College. Immense progress has been made with the development of family mediation. There are now many fine mediation services in operation in England and Wales.

People will be directed towards mediation under the terms of Section 29 of the Family Law Act. This requires that people wishing to apply for legal aid for legal representation in family matters must first attend a meeting with a mediator to determine whether mediation appears suitable for their dispute and to determine whether the person should apply for mediation instead of legal representation. As adequate quality-assured mediation services become available, this section of the Family Law Act is being implemented on an area-by-area basis. Following extensive local and national consultations, its provisions have been brought into effect in six pilot areas. These provisions will gradually be introduced throughout England and Wales. They will promote knowledge of the advantages of mediation. They will stimulate demand for mediation in family disputes.

The British Government wants mediation to become a central element in the culture of dispute resolution – a culture which will become less and less about gaining advantages over, and "scoring points" off, an ex-partner and more about making sensible, agreed arrangements for the future.

Ladies and gentlemen thank you for enabling me to give this closing address. Let me end by thanking the Council fo Europe for arranging this Conference on Family Mediation in Europe. This Conference will have played a major part in encouraging countries to establish mediation facilities and to promote a forward-looking approach to family proceedings in all our countries. It has given everyone involved a major opportunity to share the joys and the frustrations of moving towards a more modern approach to family problems. I believe that we can look forward to a future in which family disputes will be handled in a much more conciliatory manner – with mediation established as a key part of the process.

CLOSING SPEECH BY

Hans Christian KRÜGER
Deputy Secretary General of the Council of Europe

Lord Chancellor,
Excellencies, Ladies and Gentlemen,

It is an honour for me to take the floor at the end of the 4th Conference on Family Law, a two day meeting devoted to "Family Mediation in Europe".

Let me begin by once again thanking the Right Honourable the Lord IRVINE OF LAIRG, Lord Chancellor of Great Britain, for having accepted to close this Conference. We are honoured by your presence and very grateful for the excellent assessment of the work of this Conference which you have just presented.

Allow me to add here our praise for the steps being taken in the United Kingdom to promote family mediation and also for the lively and interesting role-play demonstration, showing a family mediation session, which was presented on the first day of the Conference by the UK College of Family Mediators.

Yesterday the Secretary General had the opportunity to express his gratitude to Mrs Elisabeth Guigou, Minister of Justice and "Garde des Sceaux" of France, for her opening address to this Conference. In her statement, Minister Guigou referred to the already important achievments of our Organisation in the field of family law, among which the previous Family Law Conferences, and also to the important standard setting by the Council of Europe over the years. Minister Guigou informed us of current proposals for further legislative reform in France as far as family law and mediation is concerned and we particularly welcome her support for the establishment of international mediators who would play a fundamental role in transfrontier family mediation and in minimising the risks of child abduction.

Today it is my turn to express our gratitude to the Rapporteurs for the very high quality of the reports presented and to our General Rapporteur for his valuable conclusions.

On behalf of the Council of Europe I would also like to thank the Chairpersons for their guidance during the different sessions of this Conference.

It has been pointed out, during this two day meeting, that the rapid pace of social change in recent years presents many different challenges, and difficult problems to overcome, for families and particularly for children. It has also been said that, although family mediation has been available in some of our countries for some time, it is generally a rather new phenomenon which can be organised in different ways. Mediation can be seen as an alternative dispute resolution where the judiciary is not necessarily involved but the purpose of mediation remains the same, that is: to uphold the importance of family life to children and the need for social support for parents who separate or divorce.

A successful family mediation provides crucial support to social cohesion and to the security of our citizens. In that respect, one can say that family mediation is of direct relevance for the policies of the <u>Declaration,</u> and two of the main chapters of the <u>Action Plan,</u> adopted by our Heads of State and Government on the occasion of the Council of Europe's Second Summit last October in Strasbourg. These texts call for a new strategy of **social cohesion** to respond to the challenges in society, inter alia by a programme to promote the interests of children. In another chapter of the Action Plan, calls are made to enhance the **security of the citizens**, including the protection of children suffering from inhuman treatment or different forms of exploitation.

I think you share my opinion that this 4th Conference on Family Law, both on account of the high quality of the discussions and of the record number of participants, was a success. Without doubt, this Conference has paved the way for the implementation, in Europe, of the principles contained in Recommendation No. R (98)1 on family mediation. But your debates have also given us a good basis, and much food for thought, for the continuation of our work in the area of family law in general. For this, we are very grateful and we shall do our best to ensure that maximum benefit is drawn from this Conference.

With these words I thank you for your attention and I declare the Fourth Council of Europe Conference on Family Law closed.

APPENDIX I

LISTE OF PARTICIPANTS

Sheena ADAM, Assistant Director, National Family Mediation, 9 Tavistock Place, LONDON WC1H 9SN (Tel.: 0171 383 59 93; Fax: 0171 383 59 94), UNITED KINGDOM

Ingrid ÅKERMAN, Senior Administrative Officer, National Board of Health and Welfare, 106 30 STOCKHOLM (Tel.: 46 8 783 31 63; Fax: 46 8 783 30 20), SWEDEN

Michèle AKIP, Administratrice, Conseil de l'Europe, Direction des Droits de l'Homme, Charte sociale, 67075 STRASBOURG CEDEX (Tel.: 33 3 88 41 23 46; Fax: 33 3 88 41 37 00), FRANCE

Angelo ALBERGHINI, Rue G. Servais n° 200/A-7, 10146 TURIN (Tel.: 39 11 711 456), ITALIE

Mira ALINČIĆ, Professor, Faculty of Law, Assoc. of Ministry of Labour and social Welfare, Trg. M. Tita 3, 10000 ZAGREB (Tel.: 385 1 429 222; Fax: 385 1 429 565), CROATIE

Sonia ALLES, Assistante Sociale, Caisse d'Allocations Familiales, 18, rue de Berne, 67000 STRASBOURG (Tél.: 03 88 37 68 20), FRANCE

Françoise ANCELLIN, Médiatrice Familiale, Service de l'UDAF de la Marne, 65 rue Grande Etape, 51000 CHALONS EN CHAMPAGNE (Tel.: 33 03 26 68 50 04; Fax: 33 03 26 68 50 04), FRANCE

Akira ANDO, Consul, Consultate General of Japan, "Tour Europe", 20, place des Halles, 67000 STRASBOURG (Tel.: 33 3 88 52 85 00; Fax: 33 3 88 22 62 39), FRANCE

Marie-Anne ANDRE, La Passerelle, 52, rue des Eaux Claires, 38100 GRENOBLE (Tel.: 04 76 21 99 75; Fax: 04 76 21 50 74), FRANCE

Kiyoshi AOKI, Professor of Law, Nanzan University (Japan), c/o Centre for Socio-legal Studies, University of Oxford, Wolfson College, OXFORD OX2 6UD (Tél.: 44 1865 28 42 28; Fax: 44 1865 28 42 21), UNITED KINGDOM

Christine AUBE, Chargée du Développement de la médiation, CAF du Sud Finistère, Av. Ty-Douar, 29321 QUIMPER (Tél.: 02 98 98 38 08), FRANCE

Pascal AUBERT, Responsable du Service Vie des Quartiers, Mairie d'Epinay sur Seine, 1 esplanade F. Mitterrand, 93800 EPINAY SUR SEINE (Tel.: 33 01 49 71 99 99), FRANCE

Marieta AVRAM, Directrice de la Direction de Législation et Etudes, Ministère de la Justice, 33 bd. Elisabeta, BUCAREST (Tel.: 40 1 310 01 16 / 311 07 84; Fax: 40 1 315 53 89 / 401 310 16 62), ROUMANIE

Mehlika AYTAC, Judge, The Department of International Law, Ministry of Justice, Uluslararasi Hukuk ve Dis Iliskiler Gen. Müdürlügü, ANKARA (Tel. 312 418 29 32; Fax: 312 425 02 90), TURKEY

Annie BABU, Institut Européen Médiation Familiale, 85160 ST JEAN DE MONTS, FRANCE

Ingrid BAER, Director, International Social Service, German Branch, Am Stockborn 5-7, 60439 FRANKFURT/MAIN, (Tel.: 069 95 80 74 69; Fax: 069 95 80 74 65), GERMANY

Mary BANOTTI, Member of the European Parliament, President's Mediator for transnationally abducted children, EP Brussels, 43 Molesworth St., DUBLIN 2, IRELAND

Daniel BARATHON, Responsable Permanent, Association Région Roannaise Aide aux Victimes et Médiation, 2, rue Bayard, 42300 ROANNE (Tél.: 33 04 77 72 10 26 et 33 04 77 70 97 08), FRANCE

Marie-Noëlle BARBIER, Médiateur familiale et trésorier du Centre, Centre de Médiation Familiale de Nancy, 1 rue du Manège, 54000 NANCY (Tel.: 03 83 32 05 22), FRANCE

Nathalie BARBOT, Coordinatrice-Psychologue, INTERMEDE NORD 79, 29A, Bd du Guédeau, 79300 BRESSUIRE (Tel./Fax: 05 49 81 23 72), FRANCE

Michel BARON, Psychothérapeute-Psychoanalyste, Avenir Mutualité, 50, rue de Boulainvilliers, 75016 PARIS (Tel: 33 01 45 24 57 65), FRANCE

Stéphanie BARTH, Juriste, Association Themis Maison des Associations, 1a place des Orphelins, 67000 STRASBOURG (Tel. 33 3 88 37 92 61, Fax 33 3 88 36 48 75), FRANCE

Bernadette BARTHELET, Directrice, Institut des Sciences de la famille, 30, rue Sainte Hélène, 69002 LYON (Tel: 33 4 78 92 91 24; Fax: +33 4 72 77 63 23), FRANCE

Antonietta BASSO, Psicologo Dirigente, Dipartimento Salute Mentale, Azienda per i Servizi Sanitari n° 4 Medio Friuli, Via Pozzuolo 333, UDINE (Tel.: 0432 552245; Fax: 0432 552861), ITALY

Benoit BASTARD, Sociologue, Centre National de la recherche scientifique, Centre de Sociologie des organisations, 19, rue Amélia, 75007 PARIS (Tel.: 01 40 62 65 70; Fax: 01 47 05 35 55), FRANCE

Gabrielle BASTIAN, Thérapeute de couple – Assistante sociale, Association Générale des Familles, 7 rue Sédillot, BP 4, 67064 STRASBOURG Cedex (Tel.: 03 88 21 13 82; Fax: 03 88 37 17 85), FRANCE

Ksenija BAUER, Expert Adviser, Ministry of Labour and Social Welfare, Prisavlje 14, 10000 ZAGREB (Tel.: 385 1 6169 252; Fax: 385 1 530 195), CROATIA

Anne BAUMEL, Avocat, Berverce 43B, 4960 MALMEDY (Tel.: 32 80 77 12 26; Fax: 32 80 79 31 12), BELGIQUE

Valérie BELLANGER, Service social, Crédit Lyonnais, 30, rue de Gramont, 75002 PARIS, (Tel.: 01 42 95 10 76; Fax: 01 42 95 10 90), FRANCE

Amparo BENET COBO DEL PRADO, Abogado, Pontificio Instituto Ivan Parlo II, c/ Trinitarios, 3-3°, 46003 VALENCIA (Tel.: 96 315 58 07; Fax: 96 391 81 20), ESPAGNE

Sabine BENISCH, Social Worker, Mediator, International Social Service, German Branch, Am Stockborn 5-7, 60439 FRANKFURT (Tel.: 49 69 95 80 74 66; Fax: 49 69 95 80 74 65), GERMANY

André BERNARD, Avocat à Liège, Mouvement Belge pour l'Egalité Parentale, Bd. E. de Laveleye, B-4020 LIEGE (Tel.: 32 04 343 77 07; Fax: 32 04 343 77 07), BELGIQUE

Jacques BERNOT, Président Association FLAME, Neuro Psychiatre, 8, place du Collège, 71100 CHALON SUR SAONE (Tel.: 33 03 85 46 33 06), FRANCE

Ariane BERTHY, Conseil familial Médiateur, 6, rue Jean-Paul Souturier 95300 PONTOISE
FRANCE

Jean-Pierre BERTHON, Directrice Centre de Médiation Familiale, Parentèle Association Le Cap, 8 rue Elisée Reclus, 03100 MONTLUCON (Tel.: 33 04 70 05 62 66; Fax: 33 04 70 05 62 66), FRANCE

Jos BEWER, Fonctionnaire, Ministère de la Jeunesse, Service national de la Jeunesse, B.P. 707, 2017 LUXEMBOURG (Tel. 352 478 64 64: Fax: 352 46 41 86), LUXEMBOURG

Isabelle BIERI, Présidente Autorités régionales de conciliation, Etat de Neuchâtel, rue du Château 12, 2001 NEUCHATEL (Tel.: 32 889 51 45; Fax: 32 889 62 56), SUISSE

Joël BIJAULT, Formateur, ARRFIS, Rue Guyon de Guercheville, 14200 HEROUVILLE St CLAIR, (Tel: 33 2 31 47 61 29; Fax: 33 2 31 95 68 81), FRANCE

Agneta BJÖRKLUND, Senior Administrative Officer, Ministry of Health and Social Affairs, 103 33 STOCKHOLM (Tel.: 46 8 405 34 40; Fax: 46 8 10 36 33), SWEDEN

Jacqui BLANCHARD, Manager/Mediator, Lincolnshire Family Association Service, 7 Lindum Terrace, LINCOLN LN2 5RP (Tel.: 44 01522 575700; Fax: 44 01522 575700), UNITED KINGDOM

Edward BLOOMFIELD, Head of Divorce and Mediation Branch, Lord Chancellors Dept, Selborne House, Victoria Street, LONDON (Tel.: 44 0171 210 06 85), UNITED KINGDOM

Monique BOEVER, Médiateur Familial, Centre de Consultations Conjugales, 291,, chaussée de Dinant, 5000 NAMUR (Tel.: 32 81 22 96 78; Fax: 32 81 22 96 78), BELGIQUE

Thorsten BORRAK, Junior lawyer, Hinter dem Löwen 4, 77955 ETTENHEIM (Tel.: 49 78 22 30844; Fax: 49 7822 30844), ALLEMAGNE

Maria Vittoria BORGHETTI, Médiateur familiale, Studio Legala Guerreri, Via Giotto 28, 20145 MILANO (Tel.: 02 43 90 334; Fax: 02 49 85 297), ITALIE

Hans BOSERUP, Attorney at law, mediator, adjunct professor at law, Advokatfirmaet Boserup, Højer & Christensen, Sundsmarkvej 20, 6400 SØNDERBORG (Tel.: 74 42 36 05; Fax: 74 43 44 42), DENMARK

Marie-Françoise BOSSUT, Educatrice spécialisée, Médiatrice familiale, 20/3 Résidence Les Essarts, 59110 LA MADELEINE (Tél.: 03 20 55 64 12), FRANCE

Paul BOURGEOIS, Médiateur et Formateur en médiation, Centre de recherche sur la médiation, ASBL, Centre de Médiation "A la différence" ASBL, Rue A. Buisseret 24, 4000 LIEGE (Tel.: 32 085 712961 / 32 04 253 06 15; Fax: 32 085 71 29 68), BELGIQUE

Martine BOURRY D'ANTIN, Avocat à la Cour, Membre du Conseil de l'Ordre, Représentante du Bâtonnier Madame de la Garanderie, Ordre des Avocats, 11 Place Dauphine, 75001 PARIS (Tel.: 33 01 44 32 48 13; Fax: 33 01 44 07 26 74), FRANCE

Jacqueline BROWN, Family Policy Advisor, Family Policy Division, Lord Chancellor's Department, Selborne House, 54-60 Victoria Street, LONDON SW1E 6QW (Tel.: 44 171 834 59 01; Fax: 44 171 210 87 36), UNITED KINGDOM

Ann-Christine BURMAN, Family Law Unit, Social services in Sundsvall, Norrmalmsgatan 4, 851 85 SUNDSVALL (Tel. 46 060 19 10 00; Fax: 46 060 12 61 85) SWEDEN

Pasquale BUSSO, médiateur familial, AIMS, Corso Francia 98, 10143 TORINO (Tel.: 39 11 776 78 31; Fax: 39 11 776 78 31), ITALIE

Inger BYSTRÖM, 2nd Chairman, Familjerättssocionomernas Riksförening (FSR), Seglargatan 4, 414 57 GÖTEBORG (Tel.: 46 031 85 23 04; Fax: 46 031 85 23 35), SWEDEN

Kathryn CALDWELL, Senior Teaching Fellow (Law), Law Dept, University of Essex, Wivenhoe Park, COLCHESTER, Essex CO4 3SQ (Tel.: 44 01206 872923; Fax: 44 01206 873428), UNITED KINGDOM

Laura CARDIA-VONECHE, Sociologue, Université de Genève, CMU-IMSP, 1, rue Michel Servet, 1211 GENEVE 4 (Tel.: 41 22 702 59 23; Fax: 41 22 702 59 12), SUISSE

Andrew CARTER, Ambassador, Permanent Representative of the United Kingdom to the Council of Europe, 18 rue Gottfried, 67000 STRASBOURG (Tel.: 33 3 88 35 00 78; Fax: 03 88 36 74 39), FRANCE

Elizabeth CASSELL, Senior Teaching Fellow, University of Essex, Wivenhoe Park, COLCHESTER Essex CO4 3SQ (Tel.: 44 01206 87 33 33 ext. 38 07; Fax: 44 01206 87 34 28), UNITED KINGDOM

Jean CHARRON, Educateur, Ministère de la Justice, P.J.J., 222 rue Jean Pages, 24000 PERIGUEUX (Tel.: 33 05 53 54 31 88), FRANCE

Véronique CHAUVEAU, Avocat, 91 rue de l'Université, 75007 PARIS (Tel.: 01 53 59 35 95; Fax: 01 53 59 35 99), FRANCE

Edith CHEVILLARD-VELLA, Avocat, Conseil de l'Ordre, Barreau de Lyon, 48 rue de la République, 69002 LYON (Tel. 33 4 72 40 07 17; Fax: 33 4 78 37 01 24), FRANCE

Pascale CHONIER, Travailleur social, Espace Famille –ADSEA (Association 1901), 6, rue Faidherbe, 03200 VICHY (Tel.: 04 70 32 44 78), FRANCE

Marie CILÍNKOVÁ, Member of the Czech Bar Association, Lawyer, Law Office, Bolzanova 1, 110 00 PRAHA 1 (Tel./Fax: 42 02 24 22 72 99), CZECH REPUBLIC

Nicole CLAVERIE, Responsable CIDF, Médiation Familiale, Conseillère conjugale, CIDF Belfort, 23, rue de Mulhouse, 90000 BELFORT (Tel.: 03 84 28 00 24; Fax: 03 84 23 00 24), FRANCE

Andrée COLOMER, Fonctionnaire, Ministère de la Jeunesse, Service national de la Jeunesse, B.P. 707, 2017 LUXEMBOURG (Tel. 352 478 64 64; Fax: 352 46 41 86), LUXEMBOURG

Jean-Pierre COPIN, Médiateur – Responsable du service de médiation, Association ACCORD, 38 Avenue des Vosges, 67000 STRASBOURG (Tél.: 33 03 88 24 90 80; Fax: 33 03 88 24 90 88), FRANCE

Anja CORDES, Lawyer, Sønderport, Sønderbrogade 35, 7100 VEJLE (Tel. 45 76 40 7000; Fax: 45 76 40 7002), DENMARK

Maria Rosario CORREIA DE OLIVEIRA, Juge, Tribunal Famille, Rua Marques da Fronteira, LISBONNE (Tel.: 351 1 385 39 65; Fax: 351 1 385 55 47), PORTUGAL

Bernard CORTOT, Médiateur familial, 119 rue de l'Abbaye de Vancelle, 59400 CAMBRAI (Tel.: 33 3 27 78 39 63), FRANCE

Olivier COUSTOU, Président, Chambre des Notaires des Pyrénées-Atlantiques, Maison du Notariat, 1, Avenue Alfred de Vigny, 64000 PAU, (Tel: +33 5 59 80 33 18, Fax: 33 5 59 02 77 62), FRANCE

Véronique COUSTOU, Docteur en droit, Chambre des Notaires des Pyrénées-Atlantiques, 1, avenue Alfred de Vigny, 64000 PAU (Tel.: 05 59 80 13 18; Fax: 05 59 02 7 62), FRANCE

Thierry COUZIGOU, Chef du Bureau des Affaires civiles et générales, Ministère de la Justice, 13, place Vendôme, 75001 PARIS, (Tel: 33 1 44 77 64 03, Fax: 33 1 44 77 22 76), FRANCE

Tom COX, President of the Social, Health and Family Affairs Committee of the Parliamentary Assembly of the Council of Europe

Vittorio CRISTANELLI, Law Student, University of Trento, Rotary Club Trentino Nord, Via Tambosi, 33, VILLAZZANO, 38100 TRENTO (Tel. : 39 0461 922254 ; Fax : 39 0461 233963), ITALIE

Robin ap CYNAN, Solicitor, Council Member, The Law society in England and Wales, 113 Chancery Lane, LONDON WC2A 1PL (Tel.: 0171 320 57 67; Fax: 0171 320 56 73), UNITED KINGDOM

Beata CZARNECKA-DZIALUK, Asc. Professor, Institute of Law Studies, Polish Academy of Sciences, Nowy Swiat 72 (Palac Staszica), 00-330 WARSAW (Tel.: 48 22 826 78 53; Fax: 48 22 826 78 53), POLAND

Michel DEBACQ, Conseiller technique auprès de la Ministre de la Justice, Garde des Sceaux, chargé des affaires européennes et internationales, de la coopération judiciaire internationale et des droits de l'homme, Ministère de la Justice, 13, place Vendôme , 75001 PARIS, FRANCE

Isabelle DE BAUW, Avocat-médiateur, Rue de Wynants 23, B-1000 BRUXELLES (Tel.: 32 2 548 01 88; Fax: 32 2 514 19 73), BELGIQUE

Noelle DE BRABANDERE, Juriste-Médiatrice, Infor-Droits, 87 Avenue de Boetendael, 1180 BRUXELLES (Tel.: 32 2 347 42 63; Fax: 32 2 346 74 58), BELGIQUE

Christine DE CACQUERAY VALMENIER, Médiatrice familiale en formation à l'Institut européen de médiation familiale, 108, rue d'Amiens, 60000 BEAUVAIS (Tél.:33 03 44 05 69 08), FRANCE

Véronique DELAUNAY-GUIVACH, Assistante technique, CNAF, 23, rue Daviel, 75634 PARIS CEDEX 14 (Tel.: 01 45 65 57 74), FRANCE

Christiane DELEGUE, Psychanalyste, 3 avenue de la Liberté, 67000 STRASBOURG (Tel.: 03 88 35 41 74), FRANCE

Pia DELEURAN, Lawyer, Peter Bangsvej 59, 2000 FREDERIKSBERG (Tel.: 45 38 88 11 25; Fax: 45 38 88 91 91), DENMARK

Christiane DELTEIL, Administrateur et Présidente, CNIDFF Montpellier, 7, rue du Jura, 75013 PARIS (Tél.: 33 01 42 17 12 03; Fax: 33 01 43 31 15 81), FRANCE

Jan Piet DE MAN, Médiateur familial accrédité, Institut européen pour l'intérêt de l'enfant, Ter Voortlaan 58, 2650 EDEGEM 2 (Tel.: 32 3 440 53 26; Fax: 32 3 440 53 26), BELGIQUE

Claire DENIS, Médiatrice, Association des familles d'Aunis et Saintonge, 17 rue Alcide d'Orbigny, 17000 LA ROCHELLE, FRANCE

Corinne DEWINCKLEAR, Médiateur, Centre européen de médiation, Rue des Béguinettes 69, 1170 BRUXELLES (Tel.: 32 02 673 35 06; Fax: 32 02 660 12 35), BELGIQUE

Marie-Nathalie D'HOOP, Etudiante Post-Graduat en médiation, CPSE Grivegnée, 211, rue Gretry, 4020 LIEGE (Tel.: 32 4 349 12 10), BELGIQUE

Christiane DIEMUNSCH, Médiatrice familiale, Association syndicale des Familles Monoparentales, 3, rue des Trois Epis, 68040 INGERSHEIM/COLMAR (Tel.: 33 03 89 27 09 43), FRANCE

Concette DISTEFANO, Chef du Bureau Général, Ministère des Affaires Etrangères, ROME (Tel.: 39 6 36 91 27 29; Fax: 39 6 323 59 12), ITALIE

Constance DONNARD, La Passerelle, 52, rue des Eaux Claires, 38100 GRENOBLE (Tel.: 04 76 21 99 75; Fax: 04 76 21 50 74), FRANCE

Heide DRABOWITCH, Médiateur Familiale, APME (association Père-Mère-Enfant), 36, rue des Etats Généraux, 78000 VERSAILLES (Tel.: 01 30 21 75 55; Fax: 01 39 51 28 70), FRANCE

Kirsten DREYER, Psychologist, Private Practice, Lille Østergade 8^2 , 7500 HOLSTE BRD (Tel 97 40 64 40; Fax: 97 13 22 55), DENMARK

Maryse DUFLOT, Travailleur social spécialisé, Caisse d'Allocations familiales, 76, rue Henry Dunant, B.P. 720, 59507 DOUAI CEDEX (Tél.: 33 03 27 71 35 62; Fax: 33 03 27 87 99 19), FRANCE

Igor DZIALUK, Deputy Director of judicial assistance and European law, Ministry of Justice, Al. Ujazdowskie 11, PO Box 33, 00950 WARSAW, POLAND

Marta EHLOVÁ, Member of the Czech Bar Association, Lawyer, Law Office, Mezibranská 3, 115 02 PRAHA 1 (Tel./Fax: 42 02 2221 1376), CZECH REPUBLIC

Berit EIKESET, Director, The Association of Public Family Counselling, Agencies in Norway (OFO), Markveien 35A, 0554 OSLO (Tel.: 47 22 80 61 30; Fax: 47 22 80 61 31), NORWAY

Edwige EMEGENBIRN, Membre de l'Assemblée Générale EPE, Directrice Espace/Rencontre, Ecole des Parents et Educateurs de Belgique, Rue Jean Jaurès, 6043 ROUX, (Tél.: 32 71 46 17 81), BELGIQUE

Karen ENGLUND, Social Secretary, Family Law Unit, Social services in Sundsvall, Norrmalmsgatan, 4, 851 85 SUNDSVALL (Tel. 46 060 19 10 00; Fax: 46 060 12 61 85), SWEDEN

Mark ENTIN, Représentant Permanent Adjoint de la Fédération de Russie auprès du Conseil de l'Europe, Chargée d'affaires a.i., 75, allée de la Robertsau, 67000 STRASBOURG (Tel.: 33 3 88 24 20 15/03; Fax: 33 3 88 24 19 74), FRANCE

Freya ENTRINGER, Judge, Oberlandesgericht Oldenburg, Am Flutter 2, 26655 WESTERSTEDE (Tel.: 49 04488 836 257; Fax: 49 04488 836 101), ALLEMAGNE

Martti ESKO, Secr. Gen., The Finnish Lutheran Church, The Centre of Family Issues, PL 185, 00161 HELSINKI (Tel.: 358 09 180 22 66; Fax: 358 09 180 23 61), FINLAND

Loredana ESTENSO CHAZEL, Médiatrice familiale en formation, Association neuchateloise de médiation familiale / Médiane, Rue de la Paix 73, 2300 LA CHAUX-DE-FONDS (Tel.: 032 914 18 06), SUISSE

Eugen EWIG, Rechtsanwalt / Geschaftsführer (Secrétaire Général), Bundesrechts Anwaltskammer (Barreau Fédéral Allemand), Joachimstr. 1, 53113 BONN (Tel.: 49 228 911860; Fax: 49 228 9118620), ALLEMAGNE

Clotilde FABIANI ALBERGHINI, Juge honoraire à la Cour d'Appel de Turin, Chambre pour les Mineurs, rue G. Servias n° 200/A-7, 10146 TURIN (Tel.: 39 11 711 456), ITALIE

Antonio FARINHA, Procureur de la République, Maître de Conférence sur les mineurs et le droit de la famille au Centre d'Etudes Judiciaires de Lisbonne, (Centro de Estudos Judiciarios), Largo de Limoeiro, 1100 LISBOA , PORTUGAL

Cristina FERNANDEZ ORDAS, Service for the Family, Ministry of Labour and Social Affairs, C/ Jose Abascal, 39, 28003 MADRID (Tel. : 34 91 347 81 82 ; Fax : 34 91 347 81 20), SPAIN

Ewald FILLER, Head of Department for Family Law and Children's Rights, Federal Ministry of Family Youth, Franz-Josefskal 51, VIENNA (Tel.: 43 1 534 75 245 ; Fax : 513 1679 1070), AUSTRIA

Marc FISCHBACH, Juge élu à la Cour européenne des Droits de l'Homme, 67075 STRASBOURG Cedex, FRANCE

Thelma FISHER, Director, National Family Mediation, 9, Tavistock Place, LONDON WC1H 9SN (Tél.: 44 0171 383 59 93; Fax: 44 0171 383 59 94), UNITED KINGDOM

Elisabeth FLEUREAU, Assistante sociale, Conseil Général du Bas-Rhin, Centre médico social, 23, rue Pasteur, 67600 SELESTAT (Tel.: 03 88 92 80 08), FRANCE

Marie Carla FONSECA, Procuradora da Republica, Alto Comisário para a Igualdade e a Família, Palacio Foz, Praça dos Restauradores, 1250 LISBOA (Tel.: 351 321 95 15; Fax: 351 342 91 14), PORTUGAL

Elizabeth FOSTER, Director, Family Mediation Scotland, 127 Rose Street South Lane, EDINBURGH EH2 4BB (Tel.: 44 0131 220 16 10; Fax: 44 0131 220 68 95), UNITED KINGDOM

Goulla FRANGOU, Senior Counsel of the Republic, The Law Office of the Republic, 1403 NICOSIA (Tel.: 357 2 30 22 42; Fax: 357 2 66 74 98), CYPRUS

Gerrit FRANSSEN, Assistant scientifique, Université d'Anvers, Centre de Sociologie du Droit, Grote Kauwenberg 18, B-2000 ANTWERPEN (Tel.: 32 (0)3 220 43 51; Fax: 32 (0)3 220 43 25), BELGIQUE

Marie-Françoise FUCHS, Présidente Ecole des Grands-Parents Européens, EGPE, 12, rue Chomel, 75007 PARIS (Tél.: 33 01 4 44 34 93; Fax: 33 01 45 44 33 87), FRANCE

Elisabeth GAILLY, Médiateur, Association "Médiateurs dans la Ville", 46 rue des Sablons, 78400 CHATOU (Tel.: 33 01 39 52 19 49), FRANCE

Nicole GALLUS, Avocat, Assistante à l'Université libre de Bruxelles, Association d'avocats Renchon-Vandieren-Wermer, 118, avenue Winston Churchill, 1180 BRUXELLES (Tel: 32 2 344 44 41; Fax: 32 2 347 25 58), BELGIQUE

Odile GANGHOFER, Docteur en droit, 16, rue des Pontonniers, 67000 STRASBOURG (Tél: 33 03 88 35 02 44,Fax: 33 03 88 37 12 20), FRANCE

Gabriel GARCIA-CANTERO, Professeur de Droit civil et Magistrat exc., Facultad de Derecho, Pedro Cerbuna 12, 50009 ZARAGOZA (Tel.: 34 976 76 14 26; Fax: 34 976 76 14 99), ESPAGNE

Bernadette GARIC, Vice-Présidente, AREPS Association de Réflexion et d'Entraide sur les Problèmes de Société, 17, rue des Tournelles, 75004 PARIS (Tel.: 01 42 71 68 42; Fax: 01 42 77 42 52), FRANCE

Fiona GARWOOD, Mediation Trainer and Presenter, UK College of Family Mediators, Family Mediation Scotland, 127 Rose Street, South Lane, EDINBURGH EH2 4BB, (Tel. 44 0131 220 16 10; Fax: 44 0131 220 68 95), UNITED KINGDOM

Catherine GASSEAU, Médiatrice – Médiatrice Familiale – Formatrice – "Résonances" – FCUP (Formation continue Univern. Provence), "La Musarde" Chemin du Loubortas, 13860 PEYROLLES EN PROVENCE (Tel.: 33 04 42 57 82 97), FRANCE

Friederike GEIB, Social Work trainee, International Social Service, German Branch, Am Stockborn 5-7, 60439 FRANKFURT (Tel.: 49 69 958 07 461; Fax: 49 69 95 807 465), GERMANY

Catherine GHYS, Médiatrice familiale, Espace Médiations Familiales asbl, 122, rue St Bernard, B-1060 BRUXELLES (Tel.: 32 2 537 25 44), BELGIQUE

Francesca GNECH, Law Student, University of Trento, Loc. Cernidor, 40, I-VILLAZZANO, 38100 TRENTO (Tel.: 39 0461 920899), ITALY

Renée GOBBER, Médiatrice Familiale, Association Sauvegarde de l'Enfance, 5, rue Henri Grenat, 39000 LONS LE SAUNIER (Tel.: 03 84 47 40 50; Fax: 03 84 55 06), FRANCE

Patrice GODET, Psychologue-médiateur, INTERMEDE NORD 79, 291, Bd du Guédeau, 79300 BRESSUIRE (Tel.: 33 05 49 81 23 72), FRANCE

Mariette GONIVA, Substitut Principal du Procureur d'Etat à Luxembourg, BP 15, 2010 LUXEMBOURG (Tel. 352 475981-260 ; Fax 352 460687), LUXEMBOURG

Irmgard GOTTLER-ROSSET, Advocat, BAFM, Karlstr. 41, 79104 FREIBURG (Tel.: 49 761 381 682; Fax: 49 761 381 682), GERMANY

Tacettin GÜNER, Expert in Family Research Institution, Mesrutyet cad. No. 19, ANKARA (Tel.: 90 312 419 29 79; Fax: 90 312 419 29 70), TURKEY

Caroline GRAHAM, Accredited Family Law Mediator and Convenor of CALM (comprehensive accredited lawyer mediators), 28 Queensgate, INVERNESS IV1 1YN (Tel.: 44 01463 239393; Fax: 44 01463 222879), UNITED KINGDOM

Pierre GRAND, Médiateur sauvegarde de l'enfance,Centre Médico Professionnel-Vaucluse, 25380 BELEHERBE (Tel.: 33 03 81 44 35 31; Fax: 33 03 81 44 37 76), FRANCE

Frédérique GRANET, Professeur à l'Université Robert Schuman de Strasbourg, Chargée d'études juridiques à la Commission Internationale de l'état civil (C.I.E.C.), 11, rue Victor Schoelcher, 67300 SCHILTIGHEIM, (Tel: 33 3 88 62 03 32, Fax: 33 3 88 83 07 25), FRANCE

Sylvain GRATALOUP, Maître de Conférence, Faculté de droit de l'Université P. Mendès-France, 1 rue professeur Zimmermann, 69007 LYON (Tel.: 33 04 72 72 08 12; Fax: 33 04 72 72 08 12), FRANCE

Klaus GRISEBACH, Rechtsanwalt, Arge Mediation im Dav, Badstr. 24a, 77652 OFFENBURG (Tel.: 49 0781 91670; Fax: 49 0781 916767), GERMANY

Poul GUDBERG, Lawyer, Soendergade 25, 8600 SIKKEBORG (Tel.: 45 86 82 56 00; Fax: 45 86 82 58 62), DENMARK

Haukur GUDMUNDSSON, Head of Section, Ministry of Justice, Arnarhvoll, 150 REYKJAVIK (Tél.: 354 560 90 10; Fax: 354 552 73 40), ICELAND

Gigliola GUERRERI, Avocat, via Giotto 28, 20145 MILANO (Tel.: 02 43 90 334; Fax: 39 02 4985 297), ITALIE

Marie-Françoise GUIDOLIN, Juge aux Affaires Familiales,Tribunal de Grande Instance d'Annecy, 9, rue du Rocher d'Argout, 77123 NOISY SUR ECOLE (Tel.: 01 64 24 73 52 ou 06 11 20 08 47), FRANCE

Elisabeth GUIGOU, Ministre de la Justice, Garde des Sceaux, Ministère de la Justice, 13 place Vendôme, 75001 PARIS, FRANCE

Paul GUIHARD, Président, Divorce et Médiation, 1, rue Bardoul, 49100 ANGERS (Tél.: 33 02 41 31 19 20, Fax: 33 02 41 31 15 64), FRANCE

Françoise GUIHARD, Médiatrice, Divorce et Médiation, 1, rue Bardoul, 49100 ANGERS (Tel.: 33 02 41 31 15 6; Fax: 33 02 41 31 15 64), FRANCE

Josyane GUILLEMAUT, Présidente de l'Ecole des Grands Parents des Alpes Maritimes, 63 Promenade des Anglais, 06000 NICE (Tél.: 33 04 93 44 21 59 ou 33 01 43 26 53 45; Fax: 33 01 435 435 14), FRANCE

Laurence GUILLOT, Assistante de Service Social, Département du Val de Marne, Circonscription d'Actions sanitaires et sociales, 24 bis Grande Rue Charles de Gaulle, 94130 NOGENT SUR MARNE (Tel.: 33 01 45 14 22 50; Fax: 33 01 48 77 59 54), FRANCE

Birgitte GULBRANDSEN, Adviser, Ministry of Children and Family Affairs, Postboks 8036 Dep., 0030 OSLO (Tel.: 22 24 25 19; Fax: 22 24 17 18), NORWAY

Birger HAGARD, President of the Committee on Legal Affairs and Human Rights of the Parliamentary Assembly of the Council of Europe

Danielle HANNEDOUCHE, Directrice, Alternative Médiation, 77, rue de Belfort, 33000 BORDEAUX (Tel.: 33 05 56 90 08 52; Fax: 33 05 56 93 06 88), FRANCE

Kirsten-Pia HANSEN, Lecturer at the Law School, University of Tuebingen, Law Faculty, Wilhelmstrasse 7, 72074 TUEBINGEN (Tel.: 49 7071 297 67 75; Fax: 49 70 71 29 50 44), GERMANY

Monika HARTGES, Responsible of ÖRA, ÖRA (Center of Legal Advice, aribtration and mediation), Holstenwall 6, 20355 HAMBURG (Tel.: 49 040 34 97 30 70; Fax: 49 040 34 97 36 58), GERMANY

Geneviève HARTLAND, Juriste, Divorcer autrement Espace Médiation, 21, rue des Francs Bourgeois, 67000 STRASBOURG (Tél.: 33 03 88 23 57 75), FRANCE

Marie-Thérèse HAUER, Médiatrice familiale, Association syndicale des Familles Monoparentales, 3, rue des Trois Epis, 68040 INGERSHEIM/COLMAR (Tel.: 33 03 89 27 09 43), FRANCE

Liss Unnys HAUGE, Senior executive officer in Social and Family Affairs, The County Governor of Hedmark, Fylkeshuset, 2300 HAMAR (Tel.: 47 62 54 45 66; Fax: 47 62 54 45 57), NORWAY

Pius HEEB, Juge, Landgericht, Aeulestrasse 70, 9490 VADUZ, Tel.: 075 236 65 04; Fax: 095 236 65 39), LIECHTENSTEIN

Markku HELIN, Counsellor of Legislation, Ministry of Justice, PO Box 1, 00131 HELSINKI, (Tel.: 358 9 1825 76 65; Fax: 358 9 1825 76 58), FINLAND

Martine HENRY, Association ACCORD, 38 Avenue des Vosges, 67000 STRASBOURG (Tél.: 33 03 88 24 90 80; Fax: 33 03 88 24 90 88), FRANCE

Véronique HENRY-MULLER, Educatrice spécialisée, A.D.S.E.A., 16, rue Chateaubriand, 24100 BERGERAC (Tel.: 33 05 53 27 05 13), FRANCE

Claude HERAUD, Psychologue, Président Fédération AFCC Ile de France, 10 rue de Fontenay, 94130 NOGENT SUR MARNE (Tel.: 33 01 48 73 30 92; Fax: 33 01 48 75 91 33), FRANCE

Suzanne HERBIN, Médiatrice familiale, Centre d'information sur les droits des femmes, 14, rue du Grand Chemin, 59100 ROUBAIX (Tél.: 33 03 20 70 22 18; Fax: 33 03 20 27 44 47), FRANCE

Geneviève HERINCKX, Avocat, Dreweg, 290, 1180 BRUXELLES, (Tel: 32 2 374 12 21; Fax: 32 2 374 14 41), BELGIQUE

Claus R. HESSE, Sprecher der BAFM, Bundesarbeitsgemeinschaft für Familien-mediation, Haspelstr. 24; 35037 MARBURG (Tel.: 49 64 21 25 096; Fax: 49 64 21 159 89), ALLEMAGNE

Laurent HINCKER, Avocat/Professeur associé à l'Université de Strasbourg, 11a rue du Fossé des Treize, 67000 STRASBOURG (Tel.: 33 02 88 15 14 26; Fax: 33 03 88 15 19 85), FRANCE

Magguy HOFMANS, Formatrice, A.S.B.L. MEDI-3, 112, rue Grettouheid, 4860 PEPINSTER (Tel.: 32 087 46 13 88; Fax: 32 087 46 13 88), BELGIQUE

Milan HOLUB, Chairman of the Chamber of the High Court of the Czech Republic, High Court, Vrchni Soud, Nám Hidinů 1300, PRAHA 4 (Tel.: 02 611 96 285; Fax: 02 611 96 181), CZECH REPUBLIC

The Right Honourable the Lord IRVINE OF LAIRG, Lord Chancellor of Great Britain, House of Lords, LONDON SW1A 0PW, UNITED KINGDOM

Jacqueline JANCLAES, Médiatrice familiale, Collectif contraceptions Planning, 21 A quai de l'Ourthe, 4130 TILFF (Tel. 32 04 388 28 11), BELGIQUE

Donatienne JANS, Avocat – Juriste dans les Plannings familiaux BXL, Rue d'Octobre, 20, 1200 BRUXELLES (Tel.: 32 02 763 10 77; Fax: 32 02 511 30 15) , BELGIQUE

Roland JOSSE, Médiateur familial, Ecole des parents et éducateurs de Belgique, Rue de Marbaix, 29, 6534 GOZEE, (Tél.: 32 71 21 80 50; Fax: 32 2 733 02 26), BELGIQUE

Marguerite JOURDAIN, Assistante à la Faculté de Droit de Brest, Université de Bretagne Occidentale, Saint-Germain St Martin des champs, 29600 MORLAIX (Tel.: 33 02 98 63 22 36), FRANCE

Jeannine JULLIEN-VAN de WEERDT, Médiatrice-Formatrice, Centre de Recherche sur la Médiation (C.R.M.), Rue de Clérembault, 19, 4031 LIEGE (Tel.: 32 54 367 03 02), BELGIQUE

Fériel KACHOUKH, Chargée de mission, Ministère Emploi – Solidarité, Service Droits des Femmes, 31 rue Le Peletier, 75009 PARIS (Tel.: 33 01 47 70 41 58; Fax: 33 01 42 46 99 69), FRANCE

Andranik KARAKHANOV, Adjoint au Représentant Permanent de la Fédération de Russie auprès du Conseil de l'Europe, 75 allée de la Robertsau (Tel.: 33 3 88 24 20 15/03; Fax: 33 3 88 24 19 74), FRANCE

Leyla KAYACIK, Administratrice, Conseil de l'Europe, Direction des Droits de l'Homme, Charte sociale européenne, 67075 STRASBOURG CEDEX (Tel.: 33 3 88 41 28 06; Fax: 33 3 88 41 37 00), FRANCE

Sulvie KIHL, assistant socio-éducatif, Conseil Général Equipe de Prévention spécialisée, Les Tamaris n° 415, 54100 NANCY (Tel.: 03 83 96 25 80), FRANCE

Bjorn Tore KJELLEMO, Ministry of Children and Family Affairs, Postboks 8036 Dep.0030 OSLO (Tel.: 22 24 25 19; Fax: 22 24 17 18), NORWAY

Susanna KLEINDIENST, Judge, Mediator, Prater 99, 1020 VIENNA (Tel.: 01 729 35 97; Fax: 01 72 93 597), AUTRICHE

Julien KNOEPFLER, Avocat, assistant doctorant à l'Université, Président de l'Association Médiane, Faculté de droit de l'Université de Neuchatel, 2000 NEUCHATEL (Tél.: 41 32 725 98 28; Fax: 41 32 718 12 21), SUISSE

Lone Hørup KNUDSEN, Head of Family Law Section, Government Office of Copenhagen County, Hejrevej 43, 2400 COPENHAGEN (Tel.: 45 38 17 06 89; Fax: 45 38 33 20/2), DENMARK

Sys KOCH ROVSING, Lawyer, Kvoesthusgade 3, 1251 KOBENHAVN K (Tel: +45 33 11 08 85; Fax: +45 33 93 75 30), DENMARK

Carmen KOHL-WAHL, Déléguée du Centre de Liaison et de Coordination des Services Sociaux du Bas-Rhin (CODELICO), 14, rue du Maréchal Juin, Cité Administrative, BP 1028, 67084 STRASBOURG CEDEX (Tel.: 33 03 88 76 79 91; Fax: 33 03 03 88 76 80 76), FRANCE

Cornelia KOPPER-REIFENBERG, Professeur, Katholische Fachhochschule Mainz, Schweidnitzer Str. 6, 55131 MAINZ (Tel.: 49 06 131 52 632), GERMANY

Aleksandra KORAĆ, Assist. Prof., Professor, Faculty of Law, Assoc. of Ministry of Labour andn social Welfare, Trg. M. Tita 3, 10000 ZAGREB (Tel.: 385 1 429 222; Fax: 385 1 429 565), CROATIE

Pirkko KOSKINEN, Judge, Rüstavuonen Kuja 6 D 28, 00320 HELSINKI (Tel.: 358 9 587 26 62; Fax: 358 9 587 13 27), FINLAND3

Teodora KULESEVIC, Médiateur familial, S.A.F.E., Tour Panoramique 25e étage, 54320 MAXEVILLE (Tel.: 33 03 88 95 41 30; Fax: 33 03 83 95 41 39), FRANCE

Angela LAKE-CARROLL, Chief Executive, Family Mediators Association, 1 Wyvil Court, Wyvil Road, LONDON SW8 2TG (Tel. 44 0171 720 33 36; Fax: 44 0171 720 79 99), UNITED KINGDOM

Muriel LAROQUE, Avocate à la Cour, Paris, Présidente de l'Association des Avocats de la Famille, 41, avenue Foch, 75116 PARIS (Tel.: 33 01 45 53 00 27; Fax: 33 01 47 55 06 37), FRANCE

Marianne LASSNER, Premier Juge aux Affaires Familiales, Tribunal de Grande Instance de Paris, 4 boulevard du Palais, 75001 PARIS (Tel.: 33 01 44 32 65 60; Fax: 33 01 44 32 50 52), FRANCE

Concescao LAVADINHO, Psychologue et Médiatrice familiale, Ministère de la Justice, Rua Coelho da Rocha, 48-3° Dr, 1250 LISBOA (Tel.: 351 1 397 98 11; Fax: 351 1 397 98 11), PORTUGAL

Elizabeth LAWSON, Queen's Counsel, General Council of the Bar of England and Wales, Family Law Bar Association, Cloisters, Pump Court, Temple, LONDON EWY 7AA (Tél.: 44 0171 827 40 00, Fax: 44 0171 827 41 00), UNITED KINGDOM

Micheline LAZARD, Thérapeute, Médiatrice familiale formatrice, ASBL "Autrement", 39B rue Louis Loiseau, 5000 NAMUR (Tel.: 32 081 44 03 62; Fax: 32 081 73 67 69), BELGIQUE

Vicky LEACH, Mediation Project Manager, Mediation Adviser, N.C.H. Action for Children, 231 Canferwell New Road, LONDON SE5 OTW (Tel: 44 171 701 11 14; Fax: 44 171 703 61 29), UNITED KINGDOM

Chantal LEBATARD, Administrateur, UNAF, 28, place St Georges, 75009 PARIS (Tél.: 33 01 49 95 36 18; Fax: 33 01 49 95 36 81), FRANCE

Corinne LECARPENTIER-PIERRE, Avocat, 38, rue Nationale, BP 190, 56308 PONTIVY CEDEX (Tel.: 02 97 25 21 01; Fax: 02 97 25 60 88), FRANCE

Roger LECONTE, Président, Comité National des Associations et Services de Médiation Familiale, AAJB, BP n° 8, 14111 LOUVIGNY (Tel.: 33 02 31 29 18 80; Fax: 33 02 31 29 18 89), FRANCE

Nicole LEFIEF, Intervenante Espace Rencontre, Thérapeute Familiale, Ecole des Parents et Educateurs de Belgique, Place Gambetta, 23, 6044 ROUX, (Tél.: 32 071 46 02 88), BELGIQUE

Geneviève LEGENDRE, Service Social, Crédit Lyonnais, 30, rue de Gramont, 75002 PARIS (Tel.: 33 01 42 95 10 90; Fax: 33 01 42 95 10 76), FRANCE

Annelise LEMCHE, Lawyer, Danish Family Lawyers Association, Nield Hemmingsens Gade 10, 5, BP 15, 1001 COPENHAGEN K (Tel.: 45 33 93 03 30; Fax: 45 33 93 03 10), DENMARK

Roselyne LEPLANT, Déléguée Départementale, CLICOSS de l'Hérault, 85 avenue d'Assas, 34000 MONTPELLIER (Tél.: 33 04 67 04 29 09; Fax: 33 04 67 14 19 09), FRANCE

Robert J. LEVY, William L. Prosser Professor of law, University of Minnesota, 229 19th Avenue South, Minneapolis, MN 55 455 (Tel.: 01 612 625 53 28; Fax: 01 612 625 20 11), USA

Claude LIENHARD, Avocat, 21 rue des Francs-Bourgeois, 67000 STRASBOURG (Tel.: 33 03 88 52 25 25; Fax: 33 03 88 52 25 26), FRANCE

Jytte LINDGÅRD, Advocat, N. Hemmingsensgade 10, P.B. 15, DK-1001 COPENHAGEN K (Tel.: 45 33 930 330; Fax: 45 339 303 10), DENMARK

Pirjo LIPIÄNEN, Päijät-Häme District Family Guidance and Counsel Centre, Mediator, Psychologist Family Therapist, Vuorikatu 35 B, 15100 LAHTI (Tel.: 358 3 871 050; Fax: 358 3 781 95 01), FINLAND

Rui Manuel LISBOA EPIFANIO, Procureur Général Adjoint et Auditeur Juridique auprès du Ministère de la Justice, Ministério da Justiça, Rua Nova do Almada 11 l'Esquerdo, LISBOA (Tél.: 351 1 346 56 31; Fax: 351 1 343 12 04), PORTUGAL

Mary LLOYD, Service Co-ordinator, Family Mediation Service, Block 1, Floor 5, Irish Life Centre, Lower Abbey Street, DUBLIN 1, IRELAND

Francine LOEB, Action sociale juive, 1a rue René Hirschler, 67000 STRASBOURG (Tél.: 33 03 88 35 63 57; Fax: 33 03 88 36 67 78), FRANCE

Zsuzsa LOVAS, Consultant Superviser, National Institute of Children and Family, 1134 BUDAPEST, Tüzér u. 33-35 (Tel.: 36 1 214 10 38, Fax: 36 1 465 60 27), HUNGARY

Agneta LUNDVALL, Deputy Director, Ministry for Foreign Affairs, 103 39 STOCKHOLM (Tel.: 46 8 40 55 038; Fax: 46 8 723 11 76), SWEDEN

Marisa MALAGOLI-TOGLIATTI, Professeur Universitaire, Université La Sapienza, Via dei Marsi 78, 00185 ROME (Tel.: 039 6 49 91 75 12; Fax: 039 6 445 39 39 / 445 16 67), ITALIE

Ginette MANGOT, Chef de Service et Médiatrice Familiale, Espace Famille – ADSEA, 6, rue Faidherbe, 03200 VICHY (Tel.: 33 04 70 32 44 78), FRANCE

Päivi MÄNTYLÄ-KARPPINEN, Mediator Psychologist, Family Therapist, Päijät-Häme District Family Guidance and Counseling Centre, Vuorikatu 35B, 15100 LAHTI (Tel.: 358 3 871 050; Fax: 358 3 781 95 01), FINLAND

Geneviève MANUELIAN, Département de l'Action Sociale, Centre social de Dijon, SNCF, 11, rue Mariotte, 21000 DIJON (Tel.: 03 80 40 10 64; Fax: 03 80 40 19 88), FRANCE

Benzoni MARA, Psicologa, SIMS, Via alla Valle 13, Pare, COMO (Tel.: 39 031 44 04 12; Fax: 39 031 44 04 12), ITALIE

Simon MARCOTTE, Directeur général délégué à la mission des services judiciaires, Gouvernement du Québec, Ministère de la Justice, Direction générale des services de justice, 1200 route de l'Eglise, 7ème étage, Sainte Foy, Québec (Tel: 1 418 644 77 00; Fax: 1 418 644 99 68), CANADA

Aluma MARIENBURG-WACHSMANN, Juriste, CIF-CIDF, Centre d'information des droits des femmes, 2, place du Marché-aux-poissons, 67000 STRASBOURG (Tel.: 33 03 88 32 03 22; Fax: 33 03 88 32 47 95), FRANCE

Jessica MARKWELL, Co-ordinator/Mediator, Berkshire Family Mediation, 3rd floor, 160-163 Friar Street, READING Berks (Tel: 44 11 89 57 11 59, Fax: 44 11 89 50 44 64), UNITED KINGDOM

Miquel MARTIN CASALS, Catedràtic de dret Civil / Representant de la Conselleria de Justicia, Univ. de Girona, Generalitat de Catalunya, Facultat de Dret, Universitat de Girona, Rambla Xavier Cugat 1, 17071 GIRONA (Tel.: 34 972 41 81 39; Fax: 34 972 41 81 21), ESPAGNE

Lucie MARTINEAU, Avocate chez Maître Nadal, 7, rue Oberlin, 67000 STRASBOURG (Tel.: 33 3 88 36 40 41), FRANCE

Costanza MARZOTTO, Médiateur, Professeur Univ., Centro Studi e Ricerche sulla Famiglia, Via Ariberto 8, 20123 MILANO (Tel. 39 2 832 30 81; Fax 39 2 72 34 26 42), ITALIE

Yukiko MATSUSHIMA, Professor of Law, Dokkyo University, 1-9-2 Shakujii-cho, Nerima-ku, TOKYO 177 0041 (Tel.: 81 3 39 96 46 75; Fax: 81 3 39 96 41 74), JAPAN

Gaël MATTEI, A.T.E.R. à l'Université Robert Schuman, 11, rue du Maréchal Juin, 67046 STRASBOURG Cedex (Fax: 33 03 88 14 30 24), FRANCE

Frédéric MATWIES, Formation Médiation, Association Approche des Ages, 6 rue Jean-Paul Souturier, 95300 PONTOISE (Fax: 33 01 30 38 55 92), FRANCE

Marie-Thérèse MAURICE, Médiateur familial, Maison du Droit et des Droits, Palais de Justice, 39 rue des Arènes, 39100 DOLE (Tel.: 33 03 84 72 75 47), FRANCE

Jean-Luc MAYET, Médiateur Familial, Association Sauvegarde de l'Enfance, 5, rue Henri Grenat, 39000 LONS LE SAUNIER (Tel.: 03 84 47 40 50; Fax: 03 84 55 06), FRANCE

Véronique MENAHEM, Assistante Sociale, Service Social, Crédit Lyonnais, 30, rue Gramont, 75002 PARIS (Tel.: 33 01 42 95 10 76; Fax: 33 01 42 95 10 90), FRANCE

Michel MERCADIER, Educateur Spécialisé, 6 rue du Comte du Demaine, 84000 AVIGNON (Tel.: 33 04 90 87 32 42; Fax: 33 04 90 87 32 42), FRANCE

Anne-Marie MEURIS, Médiatrice Familiale, Ecole des Parents et Educateurs de Belgique, Rue de la Vallée, 16, 6120 NALINNES (Tél.: 32 71 21 46 72; Fax: 32 2 733 02 26), BELGIQUE

Christiane MICAL, Avocat, Membre du Conseil de l'Ordre, Ordre des Avocats, Barreau de Lyon, 42 rue de Bonnel, 69484 LYON Cedex 03 (Tel. 33 4 72 60 60 09, Fax: 33 4 72 60 60 46), FRANCE

Françoise MICHAUD, Directrice Générale, CNIDFF, 7, rue du Jura, 75013 PARIS (Tél.: 33 01 42 17 12 03; Fax: 33 01 43 31 15 81), FRANCE

Anne MICHEL, Candidat Notaire, Etude Notariale St Michel - Bruxelles, Avenue van Volxem n° 157, 7190 BRUXELLES (Tel.: 32 2 414 16 17; Fax: 32 2 414 10 49), BELGIQUE

Jeannine MIGNE, Trésorière de l'AREPS, Association de Réflexion et d'Entraide sur les Problèmes de Société, 17, rue des Tournelles, 75004 PARIS (Tel.: 33 01 42 71 68 42; Fax: 33 01 42 77 42 52), FRANCE

Audra MIKALAUSKAITE, The Head of the Division of Family Policy and Equal Opportunities, Ministry of Social Security and Laobur of Lithuania, Vivulskio St. 11, 0600 VILNIUS (Tel.: 370 2 65 22 83; Fax: 370 2 65 24 63), LITHUANIA

Paul MONTGOMERY, Mediator/Prenter, UK College of Family Mediators, 47/49 Derngate, NORTHAMPTON NN1 1UF (Tel.: 44 0117 918 12 38), UNITED KINGDOM

Doris MORAWE, Rechts Anwaltin, Mediatorin (BAFM), Johanniterstr. 13, D-79014 FREIBURG (Tel.: 49 761 29 66 70), ALLEMAGNE

Marlena MOULIN, Chargée d'Etudes à la Direction de l'Action Sociale, Ministère de l'Emploi et de la Solidarité, Direction de l'Action Sociale, 11, place des Cinq Martyrs du Lycée Buffon, 75696 PARIS CEDEX 14 (Tel.: 01 44 36 96 36; Fax: 01 44 36 97 23), FRANCE

Eva MÜLLER, Pro Familia Frbg BAFM, Sundgavallee 12/10/15, 79110 FREIBURG (Tel.: 49 0761 881 11 93), ALLEMAGNE

Ihor MYSYK, Représentant Permanent Adjoint de l'Ukraine auprès du Conseil de l'Europe, 23 bd de l'Orangerie, 67000 STRASBOURG (Tel.: 33 3 88 61 44 51; Fax: 33 3 88 60 01 78), FRANCE

Eliana NICOLAOU, President of Family Court, 68 Metochiov str., 2407 NICOSIA (Tel.: 77 77 30; Fax: 357 2 66 18 90), CYPRUS

Jean-Pierre NICOLAS, Directeur du Service Social, CAES Association Trau Cotxet, 15 rue de Bruxelles, 75009 PARIS (Tel. 33 01 44 53 13 33; Fax: 33 01 44 53 13 29), FRANCE

Ewa NORDIN, Juriste au sein du Bureau du Médiateur du Président pour l'enlèvement transfrontalier d'enfants, Parlement Européen, Rue Wiertz Mon 543, 1047 BRUXELLES (Tel.: 32 2 284 46 61; Fax: 32 2 284 69 36), BELGIQUE

Inger Karin NYBORG, Leader, Family Therapy Office in Kongsvinger, Postb. 697, 2200 KONGSVINGER (Tel.: 47 628 17 855; Fax: 47 628 17 855), NORWAY

Celia OLIVARES, Secrétaire Générale, Union de Asociaciones Familiares, c/ Alberto Aguilera n° 3, 28015 MADRID (Tel.: 34 91 746 31 62; Fax: 34 91 44 590 24), ESPAGNE

Giovanna ORLANDO, Law Graduate, Via Madruzzo, 41, 38100 TRENTO (Tel.: 39 0461 981709; Fax: 39 0461 981709), ITALIE

Patrick PAQUET, Conseiller technique auprès de la Ministre de la Justice, Garde des Sceaux, chargé de la presse et de la communication, Ministère de la Justice, 13, place Vendôme, 75001 PARIS, FRANCE

Lisa PARKINSON, Director Family Mediation Training, Lawgroup U.K. and Calm Scotland, The Old House, Rectory Gardens, Henbury, BRISTOL BS10 7AQ (Tel. 44 117 950 01 40; Fax: 44 117 950 01 40), UNITED KINGDOM

Isabelle PASQUIER, Juriste –Médiatrice familiale, Ecole des Parents et des Educateurs d'Ile de France, 5 Impasse Bon-Secours, 75001 PARIS (Tel.: 33 01 44 93 44 62; Fax: 33 01 44 93 44 65), FRANCE

Catherine PELCERF, Assistante Sociale, Service Social de l'Enfance, 28 rue Salvador Allende, 92000 NANTERRE (Tel.: 33 01 56 38 26 00; Fax: 33 01 47 21 81 92), FRANCE

Christa PELIKAN, Researcher, Institut für Rechts und Kriminal soziologie, Museumstrasse 5, Postfach 1, 1016 WIEN (Tel.: 43 1 526 15 16; Fax: 43 1 526 15 16-10), AUSTRIA

Marja PELLI-NURMI, Attorney at Law, Asianajotoimisto Marja Pelli-Nurmi, Paasikivenkatu, 04200 KEROVA (Tel.: 358 9 242 35 10; Fax: 358 9 230 22 75), FINLAND

Anne-Marie PENEZ, Assistante Sociale, 187 rue St Jean, 59182 LOFFRE (Tel.: 33 03 27 91 42 45), FRANCE

Liliane PERRONE, Responsable de formation de médiation familliale, Institut de sciences de la famille, 30, rue Sainte Hélène, 69002 LYON (Tel: 33 04 78 92 91 24; Fax: 33 04 72 77 63 23), FRANCE

Myriam PICOT, Avocate, 60 rue Mazerod, 69003 LYON (Tel.: 33 04 78 60 06 94; Fax: 33 04 78 62 66 28), FRANCE

Milena PIERI, Associazione GeA Genitori ancora, via Castelfidardo, 8, MILANO (Tel./Fax: 02 29004757), ITALIE

Michel PINCEMIN, Médiateur familial, rue Charles Dornier, 25440 LIESLE (Tel.: 33 03 81 57 59 78; Fax: 33 03 81 57 59 78), FRANCE

Jörg PIRRUNG, Judge at the Court of First Instance of the Court of Justice of the European Comunities, Boulevard Konrad Adenauer, 2925 LUXEMBOURG

Emanuela PIVIDORE, Laurea Economico Giuridica Sociale, Via Morosina 38, UDINE (Tel. : 0432 28 52 82), ITALIE

Brigitte PONTHIEU, Médiatrice Familiale, 4 place de la Gare, 59500 DOUAI (Tel.: 33 03 27 96 02 05), FRANCE

Jocelyne POURVEUR, Médiatrice – Consultante – Formatrice, A.S.B.L. Medi-3, 112, rue Grettouheid, 4860 PEPINSTER (Tel.: 32 087 46 13 88; Fax: 32 087 46 13 88), BELGIQUE

Solange PUJOS, Directrice Centre de Médiation Familiale, Parentèle Association Le Cap, 8 rue Elisée Reclus, 03100 MONTLUCON (Tel: 33 04 70 05 62 66; Fax: 33 04 70 05 62 66), FRANCE

Anna E. QUIK-SCHUYT, Juge (spécialiste enfants et famille), Vice-Présidente de la Cour de 1ère instance de Utrecht, Postbus 16005, 3500 DA UTRECHT (Tel.: 31 30 691 64 28; Fax: 31 30 230 21 79), PAYS-BAS

Lawrence QUINTANO, Senior Counsel for the Republic, Office of the Attorney General, The Palace, VALLETTA (Tel. 356 23 95 75; Fax 356 24 07 38), MALTA

Jarles RAKNES, Director, Familiekontoret i Fana, The Public Family Counselling Agency in Fana (Bergen), Østre Nesttunv. 2, PB 289, 5051 NESTTUN (Tel.: 47 55 13 74 25; Fax: 47 55 13 74 29), NORWAY

Ritva RAUTIO, Mediator, Social Worker, Family therapist, Päijät-Häme District Family Guidance and Counselling Centre, Vuorikatu 35B, 15100 LAHTI (Tel.: 358 3 87 10 50; Fax: 358 3 781 45 01), FINLAND

Kirsten REIMERS-LUND, Lawyer, Member of the Council, The Danish Bar and Law Society, Kronprinsessegade 28, 1306 COPENHAGEN K (Tel.: 45 339 69 798; Fax: 45 3332 18 31), DENMARK

Anne-Claude RENAUD, Juriste, Maison du Droit et des Droits, Palais de Justice, 39, rue des Arènes, 39100 DOLE (Tel.: 33 03 84 72 75 47), FRANCE

Emile RICARD, Médiateur familial et Président R.M.A. Méditerranée, Alpha Médiations, BP 470, 84072 AVIGNON CEDEX 4 (Tel: 33 04 90 86 32 75, Fax: 33 04 90 20 14 76), FRANCE

Christopher RICHARDS, Presenter, U.K. College of Family Mediators, Flat 1, Whelan Court, Isleworth, LONDON TWY 6EG (Fax: 44 0171 391 91 65), UNITED KINGDOM

Eckart RIEHLE, Professor, Fachhochschule Erfurt, Welaienstr. 22, 7613 KARLSRUHE FRG (Tel.: 0721 84 58 07), GERMANY

Nathalie RIOMET, Magistrat, Directrice de Cabinet auprès de la Déléguée interministérielle aux droits des femmes, Présidente du Comité d'experts du Conseil de l'Europe sur le droit de la famille (CJ-FA), Hôtel de Broglie, 35, rue Saint-Dominique, 75007, PARIS (Tél : 33 01 42 75 76 21, Fax : 33 01 42 75 77 92), FRANCE

Lis RIPKE, Rechtsanwältin, Heidelberg Institute for Mediation / Universität Heidelberg, Mönchhofstrasse 11, 69120 HEIDELBERG (Tel.: 49 06221 47 12 72; Fax: 49 06 221 47 34 06), GERMANY

Martine RISSELIN, Avocat au Barreau de Bruxelles, Rue du Bailli, 49, 1050 BRUXELLES (Tel./Fax: 32 02 646 01 13), BELGIQUE

Marian ROBERTS, Assistant Director (Professional Practice and Training), National Family Mediation, 9 Tavistock Place, LONDON WC1H 9SN (Tel.: 44 0171 383 59 93; Fax: 44 0171 383 59 94), UNITED KINGDOM

Marie-Laure ROBINEAU, Conseillère technique auprès de la Ministre de la Justice, Garde des Sceaux, chargée de la politique civile et des professions judiciaires, Ministère de la Justice, 13, place Vendôme, 75001 PARIS, FRANCE

Isobel ROBSON, Partner, Andrew M. Jackson & Co. Essex House, Manor Street, HULL, East Yorkshire, HU1 (Tel.: 01482 325242; Fax: 01482 212974), UNITED KINGDOM

Annelyse ROHRBACH, Assistante sociale, Conseil Général DSSS, CMS, 11, bld de l'Europe, 67500 HAGUENAU (Tel.: 33 03 88 73 34 00), FRANCE

Ursula RÖLKE, Lawyer, International Social Service, German Branch, Am Stockborn 5-7, 60349 FRANKFURT/MAIN (Tel.: 069 95807 455; Fax: 069 95807 462), GERMANY

Dominique ROLLIN, Médiateur familiale, Centre de Médiation familiale de Nancy, 1 rue du Manège, 54000 NANCY (Tel.: 03 83 32 05 22), FRANCE

Claude ROSSIER, Directeur Institut de Médiation, Formateur-thérapeute, Vice-Président de l'Association suisse pour la médiation, C.P. 2249, 1950 SION 2 (Tel. 41 079 409 14 87; Fax: 41 027 323 14 87), SUISSE

Jenny ROWE, Principal Private Secretary of the Right Honourable the Lord IRVINE OF LAIRG, House of Lords, LONDON SW1A 0PW, UNITED KINGDOM

Joëlle RUDIN, Psychologue, Médiatrice Familiale, 40, rue des Renaudes, 75017 PARIS (Tel.: 33 01 42 67 81 07; Fax: 33 01 42 67 81 07), FRANCE

Lorna SAMUELS, Solicitor, (currently) at European Commission on Human rights, 120 rue Boecklin, 67000 STRASBOURG (Tel.: 33 03 88 31 10 56; Fax: 33 03 58 41 44 08), FRANCE

Fanta SANGARE BOUGUEON, Présidente, Association Nationale Femmes Relais Médiatrices interculturelles, 8 bis rue d'Oslo, c/o PMI d'Oslo, 93000 BOBIBNY (Tel. 33 1 48 21 11 84; Fax: 33 1 48 21 11 84), FRANCE

Petar ŠARČEVIĆ, Ambassador of the Republic of CROATIA, President of the International Family Law society, Pourtalesstr. 65, CH-3073 MURI BEI BERN (Tel.: 41 31 951 16 69), SWITZERLAND

Morten SCHAU, Mediator, Chief Psychologist, The Association of Family Counselling Agencies, Church of Norway, Storgaten 20, 0184 OSLO (Tel.: 47 22 17 09 98; Fax: 47 22 17 99 36), NORWAY

Johanna SCHIRATZKI, Senior Lecturer, The Faculty of Law, Stockholm Universitet, 106 91 STOCKHOLM (Tel.: 46 8 1627 94; Fax: 46 8 612 41 09), SWEDEN

Chantal SCHOTT, Association ACCORD, 38 Avenue des Vosges, 67000 STRASBOURG (Tél.: 33 03 88 24 90 80; Fax: 33 03 88 24 90 88), FRANCE

Andrea SCHULZ, Legal Adviser, Federal Ministry of Justice, 53170 BONN (Tel.: 49 228 58 41 17; Fax: 49 228 58 41 02), GERMANY

Werner SCHÜTZ, Director, Ministry of Justice, Bundesministerium für Justiz, Postfach 63, 1016 VIENNA (Tel. 43 1 52152 21 34; Fax: 43 1 52152 28 29), AUSTRIA

Annie SCHWARTZ, Médiatrice familiale, 3, rue du Séquoia, 78870 BAILLY (Tel.: 33 01 34 62 17 07), FRANCE

Peretz SEGAL, Director, National Centre for Mediation and Conflict Resolution, Ministry of Justice, 29 Salah Adin St., POB 1087, JERUSALEM 91010, (Tel.: 972 2 670 86 22; Fax: 972 2 586 73), ISRAEL

Annie SELLERON-PORCEDDA, Directrice de l'Association La Passerelle et médiatrice, La Passerelle, 52, rue des Eaux Claires, 38100 GRENOBLE (Tel.: 33 04 76 21 99 75; Fax: 33 04 76 21 50 74), FRANCE

George A. SERGHIDES, Judge, P.O. Box 3781, 1686 NICOSIA (Tel.: 357 2 66 18 90: Fax: 357 2 66 18 90), CYPRUS

C. France SERVOISIER, Assistante E.N., Centre d'Education Permanente de l'Université Paris X Nanterre, 200, avenue de la République, 92001 NANTERRE CEDEX, FRANCE (Tel.: 33 01 40 97 78 61; Fax: 33 01 40 97 71 81), FRANCE

Hilary SIDDLE, Solicitor, Council member, The Law Society of England and Wales, 113 Chancery Lane, LONDON WC2A 1PL (Tel.: 44 0171 320 57 67; Fax: 44 0171 320 56 73), UNITED KINGDOM

Catherine SIKINIOTIS, Psychologue, National Welfare Organisation, 12, Kyklopan rue, ATHENES (Tel.: 30 1 342 27 98; Fax: 30 1 342 27 98), GRECE

Marie SIMON, Etudiante en Médiation Familiale / Institut des Sciences de la Famille de Lyon, 48 rue de la Pierre, 69310 PIERRE-BENITE, FRANCE

Daphne-Ariane SIMOTTA, Professor at University, University of Graz, Resowi-Zentrum 4B, Institut für Zivilgerichth., Verfahren Universitätsstr. 15, 8010 GRAZ (Tel.: 043 316 380 33 47; Fax: 043 316 380 94 40), AUTRICHE

Mats SJÖSTEN, Court of Appeal Judge, Court of Appeal of West Sweden, P.O. Box 40, 401 20 GÖTEBORG, (Tel.: 46 31 701 22 00; Fax: 46 31 774 29 43), SWEDEN

Xéni SKORINI-PAPARRIGOPOULOU, Prof. Adjoint à la Faculté de droit d'Athènes, 6, rue Essopou, ATHENES (Tel.: 30 1 620 89 96; Fax: 30 1 620 89 88), GRECE

Ruth SMALLACOMBE, Chair of Family Mediators Association, The Family Mediators Association, 383 London RD, MITCHAM CR4 4BF (Tel.: 081 648 22 12; Fax: 081 648 22 12), UNITED KINGDOM

Marianne SOUQUET, Médiatrice – Formatrice, "Résonances" – Formation continue Université Provence, 220 Hameau de Pontès, 13540 PUYRICARD (Tel.: 33 4 42 92 20 10; Fax: 33 4 42 92 27 86), FRANCE

Rita STAIANO, Avvocato – Vice Présidente SIMS, SIMS – Società Mediazione Sociale, Via Gransci, 3, 88060 BADOLATO MARINA (Tel.: 0967 81 40 15; Fax: 0967 81 40 15), ITALIE

Jana ŠŤASTNÁ, Specialist, Department of Social Policy, Ministry of Labour and Social Affairs, Na Poricnim Pravu 1, 128 00 PRAHA 2, (Tel.:42 02 21 92 23 22; Fax: 42 02 299 832), CZECH REPUBLIC

Louis STEENACKERS, Notary Public (Candidate), Clementinastraat 24, 2018 ANTWERPEN (Tél.: 32 3 216 17 77; Fax: 32 3 237 01 42), BELGIUM

Werner STEINACHER, Lawyer, Verein Co-Mediation: partner of Federal Ministry for Youth and Family, A-5020 SALZBURG, Johnstrasse 11 (Tel.: 0662 88 34 73; Fax: 0662 883 47 32), AUSTRIA

Véronique STEMPFER, Thérapeute de couple – Assistante sociale, Association Générale des Familles, 7 rue Sédillot, BP 4, 67064 STRASBOURG Cedex (Tel.: 33 03 88 21 13 82; Fax: 33 03 88 37 17 85), FRANCE

Heather STEVENS, Senior Legal Assistant, Office of Law Reform (Northern Ireland Civil Service), Lancashire House, 5 Linenhall Street, BELFAST (Tel.: 353 01232 54 29 00; Fax: 353 01232 54 29 09), IRELAND

Marija STOJEVIĆ, Legal Adviser, Ministry of Labour and Social Welfare, Ministry of Labour and Social Welfare, Prisavlje 14, 10000 ZAGREB (Tel.: 385 1 6169 251; Fax: 385 1 530 195), CROATIA

Theresa STOURZH, Lawyer in family law division in Austrian Federal Ministry of the Environment, Youth and Family Affairs, A-1010 VIENNA, Franz-Josefs-Kai 51 (Tel.: 43 1 53475-224; Fax: 43 1 5131679-3041), AUSTRIA

Christoph STRECKER, Richter am Amtsgericht Stuttgart, Rosentalstr. 12, 70563 STUTTGART (Tel.: 49 711 921 32 23; Fax: 49 711 735 58 02), GERMANY

Monique STROOBANTS, Médiateur familial, Avenue du Karreveld, 5, 1080 BRUXELLES (Tel.: 32 2 414 81 81; Fax: 32 2 414 81 81), BELGIQUE

Britta SUHL, Social Worker, International Social Service German Branch, Am Stockborn 5-7, 60439 FRANKFURT (Tel.: 49 69 95 80 74 61; Fax: 49 69 95 80 74 65), GERMANY

Karin SVENNINGSEN, Lawyer, Phistersvej 12, 2900 HELERUP (Tel.: 45 3962 1987; Fax: 45 3962 0981), DENMARK

Delma SWEENEY, Family Mediation Service, Family Mediator, 1, Olney News Rathgar Ave., DUBLIN 6 (Tel.: 353 87 28 277), IRELAND

Dorrit SYLVEST NIELSEN, Head of Section, Civil Retsdirektoratet, Justitsministeriet, Æebeløgade 1, 2100 KOBENHAVN Ø (Tel. 45 33 92 33 02; Fax 45 39 27 18 89), DENMARK

Marie-Claude TALIN, Maître de Conférence, Université de Provence / FORUM Européen Formation et Recherche en Médiation Familiale, 3 place victor Hugo, 13331 MARSEILLE CEDEX 3 (Tel.: 33 04 91 28 82 59; Fax: 33 04 91 28 87 07), FRANCE

María-Mercedes TARRAZÓN RODÓN, Avocat-Médiateur, Provença, 197-199 Entresuelo, 08008 BARCELONE (Tél.: 34 93 323 31 15; Fax: 34 93 453 53 91), ESPAGNE

Doctor Sirpa TASKINEN, Head of Development, National Development and Research Centre for Welfare and Health (STAKES), Siltasaarenkatu 18A, P.O. Box 220, 00531 HELSINKI, FINLAND

Brigitte TEITLER, Médiateur familial à AADEF-MEDIATION, 4, rue Paul Eluard, 93000 BOBIGNY (Tel.: 33 01 48 30 21 21; Fax: 33 01 48 30 01 81), FRANCE

Annie TEL-BOÏMA, Médiateur, Présidente des Ateliers de la Médiation, 2 Passage de la Teille, 38240 MEYLAN (Tel.: 33 04 76 90 58 62), FRANCE

Laura Maria TELES DE BARROS, Assistante sociale, médiatrice familiale, Gabinete de mediaçâo familiar, rua Carlos Wallenstein n° 12, 2° Esq., 2795 Caruaxide, (Tel. 351 09 41 85 380), PORTUGAL

Jacqueline TEPAZ, Vice-Président de la Chambre de la famille au TGI de Chalons en Champagne, 2 quai Eugène Perrier, 51000 CHALONS EN CHAMPAGNE (Tel.: 33 03 26 69 27 01; Fax: 33 03 26 69 27 45), FRANCE

Marie THEAULT, Thérapeute et Médiatrice familiale, 2, allée des Crêtes, 14210 BARON/ODON (Tel.: 33 02 31 26 05 21; Fax: 33 02 31 26 05 21), FRANCE

Aline THILLY, Chercheur en médiation familiale, Université libre de Bruxelles, Faculté de droit CP 137, 50 avenue F.D. Roosevelt, 1050 BRUXELLES (tél: 32 2 650 45 57, Fax: 32 2 374 84 48), BELGIQUE

Anne-Marie THOMA, Chargée de la direction du Service de guidance de l'enfance, Ministère de l'Education Nationale et de la Formation Professionnelle, Ministre aux Handicapés et aux Accidentés de la Vie, 38, rue de la Libération, 4210 ESCH/ALZETTE (Tel.: 352 54 04 72; Fax: 352 54 04 73), LUXEMBOURG

Gabriela THOMA-TWAROCH, judge for family affairs, District Court Döbling in Vienna, c/o Bezirksgericht Döbling, Obersteinergasse 20-22, 1190 WIEN, AUSTRIA

Hellen THORUP, Advokat, Danish Law Society, Gammeltorv 6, Postboks 2004, 1011 KØBENHAVN K (Tel.: 45 33 14 70 70; Fax: 45 33 15 05 70), DENMARK

Marie-Christine THOUVENOT, Médiateur familiale, Centre de Médiation Familiale de Nancy, 1 rue du Manège, 54000 NANCY (Tel.: 03 83 32 05 22), FRANCE

Dominique TOUTAIN, La Passerelle, 52, rue des Eaux Claires, 38100 GRENOBLE (Tel.: 33 04 76 21 99 75; Fax: 33 04 76 21 50 74), FRANCE

Charlotte TROCK, Principal, Government Office of Copenhagen County, Hejrevej 43, 2400 COPENHAGEN N.V. (Tel.: 45 38 17 06 37; Fax: 45 38 33 20 12), DENMARK

Vito TUMMINO, Psycologo, SIMS, Via Collina 3, COMO (Tel.: 39 031 52 33 27; Fax: 39 031 58 57 61), ITALIE

Agnès VALANCOGNE, Médiatrice familiale, Association d'Information, d'Education et de Conseil Familial, 7 ter rue de Champagny, 71120 CHAROLLES, FRANCE (Tel.: 33 03 85 24 17 25; Fax: 33 03 85 88 35 56), FRANCE

Jacques VAN DAMME, Président (EPE) et Vice-Président (FIEP), Ecole des Parents et Educateurs de Belgique + FIEP, Rue Berkendael 132, BTE 11, 1050 BRUXELLES, (Tel.: 32 2 344 36 15; Fax: 32 2 344 36 15), BELGIQUE

Hélène VAN DEN STEEN, Médiatrice et Professeur, Centre Européen de Médiation ASBL, 119, rue Hôtel des Monnaies, 1060 BRUXELLES (Tél./Fax: 32 2 537 34 15), Institut supérieur de Promotion sociale Communauté française, 84, rue de Boussu, 7370 DOUR (Mons) Tél.: 32 65 65 24 47), BELGIQUE

Benoît VAN DIEREN, Médiateur familial, Ecole des parents et éducateurs de Belgique, Avenue du Bel Horizon, 11, 1310 LA HULPE (Tél.: 32 2 654 17 24; Fax: 32 2 733 02 26), BELGIQUE

Isabelle VAN KERCKHOVE, Médiatrice familiale-Juriste, Renaat de Rudderlaan 22, 2650 EDEGEM (Tel.: 32 3 457 99 28), BELGIQUE

Ann VAN PELT, Membre de la Direction, Steunpunt Algemeen Welzynswerk, Diksmuidelaan 50, 2600 BERCHEM (Tel.: 32 3 366 15 40; Fax: 32 3 366 11 58), BELGIQUE

Monique VARD, Médiatrice familiale, Caisse d'Allocations Familiales du P. de D., Cité administrative, Rue Pélissier, 63032 CLERMONT FERRAND (Tel.: 33 04 73 37 30 04, Fax: 33 04 73 42 86 65), FRANCE

Evelyne VINK, Médiatrice familiale, Ecole des parents et éducateurs de Belgique, Avenue de la Tenderie, 23, 1170 BRUXELLES (Tél.: 32 2 660 40 47; Fax: 32 2 733 02 26), BELGIQUE

Giovanni VOLPE, Juge honoraire, Association Italienne Juges des enfants près du Tribunale per minorenni, Via dei Bresciani 32, 00186 ROMA (Tel.: 39 06 88 93255; Fax: 39 06 688 92 766), ITALIE

Bernt WAHLSTEN, Chairman Familjerättssocionomernas Riksförening (FSR), Seglargatan 4, 414 57 GÖTEBORG (Tel.: 46 031 85 23 04; Fax: 46 031 85 23 35), SWEDEN

Janet WALKER, Professor, Director of the Newcastle Centre for Family Studies, University of Newcastle upon Tyne, Claremont Bridge, NEWCASTLE UPON TYNE NE1 7RU, UNITED KINGDOM

Elisabeth WALSH, Chief Executive, U.K. College of Family Mediators, 24-32 Stephenson Way, LONDON NW1 2HX (Tel. 44 0171 391 91 62; Fax: 44 0171 391 91 65), UNITED KINGDOM

Alexandre WANET, Etudiant en médiation, IEPS Dour/Centre Européen de Médiation Bxl, 20, Av. des Lauriers, 4053 EMBOURG (Tel.: 32 4 365 64 77), BELGIQUE

Marie-Thérèse WERSCHNER, Enquêtrice spécialisée auprès des Tribunaux et médiatrice familiale, 8, rue de Turckheim, 68000 COLMAR (Tél.: 33 3 89 79 46 70), FRANCE

Véronique WERVER, Association ACCORD, 38 Avenue des Vosges, 67000 STRASBOURG (Tél.: 33 03 88 24 90 80; Fax: 33 03 88 24 90 88), FRANCE

Sarah WHITE, Family Mediation Project Manager, Legal APD Board, Head Office, 85 Grays inn Road, LONDON WC1X 8AA (Tel.: 44 0171 831 35 87; Fax: 44 0171 813 53 30), UNITED KINGDOM

Anita WICKSTRÖM, Deputy Director, Ministry of Justice, Department for Business and Family Law, 103 33 STOCKHOLM (Tel. 46 8 405 4694; Fax 46 8 405 4395), SWEDEN

Eva WIEDERMANN, Psychologist Mediator, Verein Co-Mediation, partner of Federal Ministry for Youth and Family, Othmarg. 23, 1200 WIEN (Tel.: 0664 101 11 59; Fax: 01 263 22 30 / 150), AUTRICHE

Nicholas WILSON, High Court Judge, Family Division, Royal Courts of Justice, Strand, LONDON WC2 (Tel. 44 0171 936 66 79 / 44 0171 221 36 34, Fax: 44 0171 936 74 43; Fax 44 0171 727 31 21), UNITED KINGDOM

Renate WINTER, Judge, at present consultant at the Centre for International Crime Prevention, United Nations, Lagergasse 6/8, 1030 WIEN, (Tel: 43 1 21 345 56 91 ; Fax : 43 12 13 45 58 98), AUSTRIA

Stephane WINTER, Juge aux affaires familiales, TGI, 2 quai E. Perrier, 51000 CHALONS EN CHAMPAGNE (Tel. : 33 03 26 69 36 91 ; Fax : 03 26 69 27 45), FRANCE

Ronit ZAMIR, Legal Adviser, The National Center for Mediation and Conflict Resolution, Ministry of Justice, 29 Salah a-Din St., JERUSALEM (Tel. : 02 670 86 22 ; Fax : 02 586 94 73 ; Fax : 03 5277 276), ISRAEL

Victor ZAMMIT, Director, Department of Family Welfare, 469, St Joseph High Road, St VENERA HMR 1S(Tel. : 356 44 34 15, Fax : 356 447 011), MALTA

Luis ZARRALUQUI, Président de l'Association espagnole d'avocats de famille et vice-Président de 'International Academy of Matrimonial lawyers' (European Chapter), P° Pintor Rosales, 82-1° DCHA, 28008 MADRID (Tel: 34 91 549 39 63/14; Fax: +34 91 549 36 22), ESPAGNE

Robert ZEGADZO, Judge, Ministry of Justice, Al. Ujazdowskie 11, 00 950 WARSAW (Tel.: 48 22 622 08 81; Fax: 48 22 628 89 32), POLOGNE

SECRETARIAT

Daniel TARSCHYS, Secrétaire Général/Secretary General

Hans Christian KRÜGER, Secrétaire Général Adjoint/Deputy Secretary General

Marie-Odile WIEDERKEHR, Directrice Adjointe des Affaires Juridiques/Deputy Director of Legal Affairs

Margaret KILLERBY, Chef de la Division du droit privé, Direction des Affaires Juridiques/Head of the Division of Private Law, Directorate of Legal Affairs

Carlos de SOLA, Chef de la section bioéthique, Division du droit privé, Direction des Affaires Juridiques/Head of the Bioethics section, Division of Private Law, Directorate of Legal Affairs

Marta REQUENA, Administrateur, Division du droit privé, Direction des Affaires Juridiques/Administrative Officer, Division of Private Law, Directorate of Legal Affairs

Jean CLAUS, Assistant administratif principal, Division du droit privé, Direction des Affaires Juridiques/Principal Administrative Assistant, Division of Private Law, Directorate of Legal Affairs

Lucy ANCELIN, secrétaire, Division du droit privé, Direction des Affaires Juridiques/Secretaary, Division of Private Law, Directorate of Legal Affairs

Marie-Luce DAVIES, secrétaire, Division du droit privé, Direction des Affaires Juridiques/Secretaary, Division of Private Law, Directorate of Legal Affairs

Elisabeth HEURTEBISE, secrétaire, Division du droit privé, Direction des Affaires Juridiques/Secretaary, Division of Private Law, Directorate of Legal Affairs

Interprètes/interpreters

Derrick WORSDALE
Amath FAYE
Isabelle MARCHINI

APPENDIX II

RECOMMENDATION No. R (98) 1,
ADOPTED BY THE COMMITTEE OF MINISTERS
OF THE COUNCIL OF EUROPE
ON 21 JANUARY 1998,
AND EXPLANATORY MEMORANDUM

The Third European Conference on family law on the subject "Family Law in the future" (Cadiz, 20-22 April 1995) recommended that the Council of Europe give consideration to the question of family mediation or other processes to resolve family disputes in the light of the conclusions of this conference. It also recommended that the Council of Europe examine the possible preparation of an international instrument containing principles on mediation or other processes to resolve family disputes.

Following this proposal, the Committee of Experts on Family Law (CJ-FA), under the authority of the European Committee on Legal Co-operation (CDCJ), was instructed to consider principles relating to mediation or other processes to resolve family disputes. In order to carry out its terms of reference, the CJ-FA set up the Working Party on Mediation and Other Processes to Resolve Family Disputes (CJ-FA-GT2). The latter prepared a draft recommendation and draft explanatory memorandum on family mediation. During its 30th meeting, the CJ-FA completed its work on these texts, which were subsequently revised by the representatives of the fourty member states of the Council of Europe in the CDCJ. On 21 January 1998 the Committee of Ministers adopted Recommendation No. (98) 1 on family mediation and authorised the publication of its explanatory memorandum.

Recommendation No. R (98) 1
of the Committee of Ministers to member states
on family mediation
(Adopted by the Committee of Ministers on 21 January 1998
at the 616th meeting of the Ministers' Deputies)

1.   The Committee of Ministers, under the terms of Article 15.b of the Statute of the Council of Europe,

2.   Recognising the growing number of family disputes, particularly those resulting from separation or divorce, and noting the detrimental consequences of conflict for families and the high social and economic cost to states;

3.   Considering the need to ensure the protection of the best interests and welfare of the child as enshrined in international instruments, especially taking into account problems concerning custody and access arising as a result of a separation or divorce;

4.   Having regard to the development of ways of resolving disputes in a consensual manner and the recognition of the necessity to reduce conflict in the interest of all the members of the family;

5.   Acknowledging the special characteristics of family disputes, namely:

–   the fact that family disputes involve persons who, by definition, will have interdependent and continued relationships;

–   the fact that family disputes arise in a context of distressing emotions and increase them;

–   the fact that separation and divorce impact on all the members of the family, especially children;

6.   Referring to the European Convention on the Exercise of Children's Rights, and in particular to Article 13 of this convention, which deals with the provision of mediation or other processes to resolve disputes affecting children;

7.   Taking into account the results of research into the use of mediation and experiences in this area in several countries, which show that the use of family mediation has the potential to:

–   improve communication between members of the family;

–   reduce conflict between parties in dispute;

–   produce amicable settlements;

–   provide continuity of personal contacts between parents and children;

–   lower the social and economic costs of separation and divorce for the parties themselves and states;

–   reduce the length of time otherwise required to settle conflict;

8.   Emphasising the increasing internationalisation of family relationships and the very particular problems associated with this phenomenon;

9.   Realising that a number of states are considering the introduction of family mediation;

10.   Convinced of the need to make greater use of family mediation, a process in which a third party, the mediator, impartial and neutral, assists the parties themselves to negotiate over the issues in dispute and reach their own joint agreements,

11.   Recommends the governments of member states:

i.   to introduce or promote family mediation or, where necessary, strengthen existing family mediation;

ii.   to take or reinforce all measures they consider necessary with a view to the implementation of the following principles for the promotion and use of family mediation as an appropriate means of resolving family disputes.

Principles of family mediation

I. Scope of mediation

a.   Family mediation may be applied to all disputes between members of the same family, whether related by blood or marriage, and to those who are living or have lived in family relationships as defined by national law.

b.   However, states are free to determine the specific issues or cases covered by family mediation.

II. Organisation of mediation

a.   Mediation should not, in principle, be compulsory.

b.   States are free to organise and deliver mediation as they see fit, whether through the public or private sector.

c.   Irrespective of how mediation is organised and delivered, states should see to it that there are appropriate mechanisms to ensure the existence of:

–   procedures for the selection, training and qualification of mediators;

–   standards to be achieved and maintained by mediators.

161

III. Process of mediation

States should ensure that there are appropriate mechanisms to enable the process of mediation to be conducted according to the following principles:

i.   the mediator is impartial between the parties;

ii.   the mediator is neutral as to the outcome of the mediation process;

iii.   the mediator respects the point of view of the parties and preserves the equality of their bargaining positions;

iv.   the mediator has no power to impose a solution on the parties;

v.   the conditions in which family mediation takes place should guarantee privacy;

vi.   discussions in mediation are confidential and may not be used subsequently, except with the agreement of the parties or in those cases allowed by national law;

vii.   the mediator should, in appropriate cases, inform the parties of the possibility for them to use marriage counselling or other forms of counselling as a means of resolving their marital or family problems;

viii.   the mediator should have a special concern for the welfare and best interests of the children, should encourage parents to focus on the needs of children and should remind parents of their prime responsibility relating to the welfare of their children and the need for them to inform and consult their children;

ix.   the mediator should pay particular regard to whether violence has occurred in the past or may occur in the future between the parties and the effect this may have on the parties' bargaining positions, and should consider whether in these circumstances the mediation process is appropriate;

x.   the mediator may give legal information but should not give legal advice. He or she should, in appropriate cases, inform the parties of the possibility for them to consult a lawyer or any other relevant professional person.

IV. The status of mediated agreements

States should facilitate the approval of mediated agreements by a judicial authority or other competent authority where parties request it, and provide mechanisms for enforcement of such approved agreements, according to national law.

V. Relationship between mediation and proceedings before the judicial or other competent authority

a.   States should recognise the autonomy of mediation and the possibility that mediation may take place before, during or after legal proceedings.

b.   States should set up mechanisms which would:

i   enable legal proceedings to be interrupted for mediation to take place;

ii.   ensure that in such a case the judicial or other competent authority retains the power to make urgent decisions in order to protect the parties or their children, or their property;

iii.   inform the judicial or other competent authority whether or not the parties are continuing with mediation and whether the parties have reached an agreement.

VI. Promotion of and access to mediation

a.   States should promote the development of family mediation, in particular through information programmes given to the public to enable better understanding about this way of resolving disputes in a consensual manner.

b.   States are free to establish methods in individual cases to provide relevant information on mediation as an alternative process to resolve family disputes (for example, by making it compulsory for parties to meet with a mediator), and by this enable the parties to consider whether it is possible and appropriate to mediate the matters in dispute.

c.   States should also endeavour to take the necessary measures to allow access to family mediation, including international mediation, in order to contribute to the development of this way of resolving family disputes in a consensual manner.

VII. Other means of resolving disputes

States may examine the desirability of applying, in an appropriate manner, the principles for mediation contained in this recommendation, to other means of resolving disputes.

VIII. International matters

a.   States should consider setting up mechanisms for the use of mediation in cases with an international element when appropriate, especially in all matters relating to children, and particularly those concerning custody and access when the parents are living or expect to live in different states.

b.   International mediation should be considered as an appropriate process in order to enable parents to organise or reorganise custody and access, or to resolve disputes arising following decisions having been made in relation to those matters. However, in the event of an improper removal or retention of the child, international mediation should not be used if it would delay the prompt return of the child.

c.   All the principles outlined above are applicable to international mediation.

d.   States should, as far as possible, promote co-operation between existing services dealing with family mediation with a view to facilitating the use of international mediation.

e.   Taking into account the particular nature of international mediation, international mediators should be required to undergo specific training.

Explanatory memorandum

A. General considerations

1.	The Third European Conference on family law on the subject "Family Law in the Future" (Cadiz, Spain, 20-22 April 1995) recommended that the Council of Europe give consideration to the question of family mediation or other processes to resolve family disputes in the light of the conclusions of this conference, and examine the possible preparation of an international instrument containing principles relating to mediation or other processes to resolve family disputes.

2.	Following this proposal, the Committee of Experts on Family Law (CJ-FA), under the authority of the European Committee on Legal Co-operation (CDCJ), was instructed "to draw up a report on principles relating to mediation or other processes to resolve family disputes and, if appropriate, to make proposals to the CDCJ concerning the possible preparation of an international instrument in this field". In order to carry out its terms of reference, the CJ-FA set up the Working Party on Mediation and Other Processes to Resolve Family Disputes (CJ-FA-GT2).

3.	The Working Party on Mediation and Other Processes to Resolve Family Disputes, under the authority of the CJ-FA, held three meetings at which it proposed a draft recommendation on family mediation. The CJ-FA completed its work on the draft recommendation during its 30th meeting which was subsequently revised by the CDCJ and adopted by the Committee of Ministers on 21 January 1998 as Recommendation No. R (98) 1.

B. Comments on the recommendation

4.	The use of family mediation and other dispute resolution processes related to family matters, as alternatives to judicial or administrative decision-making, is a relatively new process in the member states of the Council of Europe and there is no international legal instrument which established the main directions concerning family mediation as well as the basic principles applicable to this process of dispute resolution. Therefore, the aim of Recommendation No. R (98) 1 is to fill this gap, and above all to assist and provide states with a basis and framework for the establishment and regulation of the alternative processes for the resolution of family disputes, within a number of guiding principles.

5.	This recommendation deals with systems relating to the resolution of family disputes, particularly those arising during the process of separation and divorce, in order:

a.	to promote consensual approaches, thereby reducing conflict in the interest of all family members;

b.	to protect the best interests and welfare of children in particular by reaching appropriate arrangements concerning custody and access;

c.   to minimise the detrimental consequences of family disruption and marital dissolution;

d.   to support continuing relationships between family members, especially those between parents and their children;

e.   to reduce the economic and social costs of separation and divorce, both to families and to states.

6.   Extensive academic research on the nature and impact of family disputes shows that ongoing conflicts can undermine parenting abilities and cause significant difficulties for children. In high conflict families, when communication between family members is at its poorest, more prolonged disturbance may develop. As a result, a heavy responsibility is placed on those seeking to settle disputes which can otherwise escalate in the intense emotional context of separation and divorce.

7.   Research in Europe, North America, Australia and New Zealand suggests that family mediation is better suited than more formal legal mechanisms to the settlement of sensitive, emotional issues surrounding family matters. Reaching agreements in mediation has been shown to be a vital component in making and maintaining co-operative relationships between divorcing parents: it reduces conflict, and encourages continuing contact between children and both their parents. Parents who are able to make their own decisions about arrangements for the residence of their children, and for contact between children and the non-residential parent, are more likely to make these arrangements work and less likely to ignore or break them. It is known that many parents experience difficulties in complying with decisions which are imposed by the judicial or other competent authority, thus causing further disputes and an unsatisfactory situation for children, whereas decisions reached consensually by the parents have a better chance of standing the test of time, thus protecting the best interests of children.

8.   Furthermore, if agreements can be reached in mediation, there is the possibility that the complexity and duration of any subsequent legal proceedings may be reduced. This can have the effect of reducing the financial costs associated with the divorce process, particularly those related to the costs of the legal proceedings. The reduction of costs should not, therefore, be considered to be the principal rationale for promoting mediation as an alternative dispute resolution process. Rather, the reduction of costs should be seen as an important benefit when it is achieved.

9.   In any event, although providing empirical evidence is not straightforward, there is general consensus that reducing conflict and improving communication in families which are disrupted by marital separation and divorce results in significant benefits which reduce the social and psychological costs, reflected in improved well-being, physical and mental health, and work and school performance. By contrast, unresolved disputes can cause severe stress, which in turn may undermine or threaten the stability of the separated family, new adult attachments, remarriage, and stepfamily life.

10. Having regard to the United Nations Convention on the Rights of the Child, and the European Convention on the Exercise of Children's Rights, the Committee of Experts on Family Law (CJ-FA) noted:

a. the principles and standards for treatment of children, for laws, policies and practice which affect children and for both formal and informal relationships with children;

b. the importance of family life to children and the need for broad social support for both parents, as they each have common responsibilities for the upbringing of children;

c. that in the event of conflict it is desirable for families to try to reach agreement before bringing the matter before a judicial or other competent authority;

d. the great emphasis placed on the importance of recognising children as people with human rights, and of facilitating the exercise of these rights by ensuring that children are themselves, or through others, informed of, and allowed to participate in, family proceedings which affect them, and in particular, in matters involving the exercise of parental responsibilities such as residence of, and access to, children. It is expected that due weight should be given to the views expressed by the child;

e. that mediation and other processes to resolve disputes should be encouraged.

11. During the work which led to the preparation of the recommendation, it was acknowledged that concerns about the increasing number of marriages ending in divorce have led states to introduce and support a variety of means of resolving family disputes amicably. Not all of these are referred to specifically as "family mediation", although their aims and objectives may be similar. These methods may include, for instance, conciliation, conciliation counselling,1 family counselling, and so on. These processes are likely to have a number of characteristics in common with family mediation: for example, they usually involve bringing the parties together to talk through their difficulties and disputes; they normally involve a skilled professional facilitating the discussions; and their aim is to help the parties reach solutions amicably.

12. In order to examine the various aspects and issues concerning the use of family mediation as a means of resolving disputes in a consensual manner, information was requested from member states of the Council of Europe and subsequently a report was prepared for the CJ-FA.

a. Overall, family mediation as an alternative dispute resolution process is relatively new in many states, with certain states having no such process available.

b. In certain states there are provisions for family mediation during separation and divorce. While the emphasis in all of them is on making arrangements for children (i.e. custody and access matters), in nearly all

167

states, parties may settle other disputes, such as those relating to finance and property, with mediation.

c.   Mediation is considered to be a process which parties should enter voluntarily. In Norway it is compulsory to meet with a mediator before separation or divorce proceedings, or as a prerequisite for court proceedings regarding parental responsibilities, custody or access.

d.   In all states, parties retain the right to seek independent legal advice, but lawyers usually do not attend mediation.

13.   It would appear that where family mediation has been, or is being, introduced, the ways in which it is developing are consistent across states. Mediation is developing both within legal proceedings and extra-judicially.

14.   For the most part, in states where mediation has been developed, the principles in the recommendation are already being upheld. This recommendation encourages states to develop and extend alternative means of amicable dispute resolution and mediation, and to consider the desirability of applying the principles of the recommendation to them.

15.   Family disputes have a number of special characteristics which must be taken into account in mediation:

a.   there are usually continuing and interdependent relationships. The dispute settlement process should facilitate constructive relationships for the future in addition to enabling the resolution of current disputes;

b.   family disputes usually involve emotional and personal relationships in which feelings can exacerbate the difficulties, or disguise the true nature of the conflicts and disagreements. It is usually considered appropriate for these feelings to be acknowledged and understood by parties and by the mediator;

c.   disputes which arise in the process of separation and divorce impact on other family members, notably children who may not be included directly in the mediation process, but whose interests may be considered paramount and therefore relevant to the process.

16.   This recommendation considers mediation to be a process in which a third party, who has no vested interest in the matters in dispute, facilitates discussion between the parties in order to help them to resolve their difficulties and reach agreements. Mediation is not a new process – it has been used for a long time in traditional societies for the resolution of disputes within communities and kinship systems, and more recently in western societies for the resolution of industrial disputes. Mediation is considered to have a number of unique characteristics: in particular, the mediator has no authority to impose a solution on the parties but should remain both neutral and impartial. The mediator's role is to help the parties negotiate together and to reach their own joint agreements. The mediator is not expected to give advice to the parties, particularly legal advice which remains the proper remit of independent lawyers who may be appointed by each party to represent his

or her individual interests. It is not the role of the mediator to influence the decision-making process, nor to put pressure on the parties to reach any particular agreement. Agreements reached under pressure are more likely to be disregarded and broken.

17.   Also, because it is an important principle that parties should enter mediation voluntarily, they should be willing to mediate their disputes. Research has demonstrated that pressure to mediate against the will of one or all parties is not effective and may increase hostility. Making it compulsory for parties to meet with a mediator to explore the relevance and benefits of mediation is not inconsistent with this principle.

18.   It is now commonly accepted that more traditional legal processes are not well suited to the resolution of sensitive, emotional issues in family disputes, and that mediation offers a more constructive approach.

19.   Notwithstanding the desirability of promoting amicable settlements, the development of mediation and other alternative means of dispute resolution should not prevent every citizen's right of access to justice. The judicial or other competent authority in each state exists to protect its citizens and to ensure that principles of fairness, justice and due process are applied at all times and in all aspects of family law.

20.   The increasing internationalisation of family relationships renders it important to create a mechanism for co-operation between states and to encourage the use of mediation and other means of resolving disputes, when parents are living or expect to live in different states, in all matters relating to children, and in particular to resolve disputes which may arise in respect of transfrontier access and custody issues.

21.   Mediation has been used as a preferred method of dispute resolution in many international conflicts, particularly between governments. In principle, then, there is every reason to believe that family disputes with an international dimension should be amenable to mediation. Although there is relatively little experience of international mediation in Europe, a body of mediators in France has substantial experience of mediation in child abduction cases across Europe and mediators in other states are extending their skills in this area. In North America, inter-state or US-Canadian divorce disputes are commonly mediated despite wide variations in divorce legislation and procedures, and much can be learned in Europe from this experience.

C. Comments on the principles

Principle I: Scope of mediation

22.   As its name implies, family mediation deals primarily with disputes between members of the same family. This does not prevent states from setting up, should they so wish, mediation systems designed to resolve disputes between the state and the individual. However, when mediation is used in the non-private sphere, the state should take account of the interests of children and comply with its duty to protect them. In any event the mediator

should ensure that the child is not at risk (see paragraph 42 below) and that the child is informed about the mediation in appropriate cases (see paragraph 45 below).

23.   The notion of family is a broad one, going beyond the family unit based on blood or marriage ties, so as to give states greater latitude and enable them to include family situations as defined in their respective domestic legislation.

24.   It is generally accepted that all aspects of a family dispute should be open to consideration during the mediation process. In order to ensure realistic and appropriate application of mediation, states are free to determine the specific issues or cases covered by family mediation. Some states, for example, may wish to limit mediation to aspects of the dispute which are justiciable or to problems concerning separation and divorce.

25.   Mediation in separation and divorce normally includes disputes relating to:

–   custody: where and with whom a child should reside (the notion of "custody" is increasingly referred to as "residence")

–   access: the contact the child may have with the parent who is no longer living with the child on a daily basis, or with other close family members such as grandparents (the notion of "access" is increasingly referred to as "contact")

–   economic matters: the assets available, and how these might be shared by the parties to meet their own respective needs and circumstances after divorce; dispositions concerning the matrimonial home and its contents.
In the course of mediating these issues, however, arrangements for children's education and health and for contact with wider kinship networks may be discussed, and agreements reached.

26.   To avoid injustice or to protect one or more family members, states may wish to limit the use of family mediation in certain circumstances. Research shows that, where there have been incidents of domestic violence or threats to the safety of one partner by the other, mediation may not be suitable. Discussions in mediation should always be conducted in a safe atmosphere without fear of harm or intimidation.

Principle II: Organisation of mediation

27.   It is generally agreed that mediation is an alternative means of resolving disputes which must be entered into voluntarily by each party. Research shows that enforced mediation can result in agreements being made which are not necessarily reached through consensual decision-making. Such agreements are less likely to be long-lasting.

28.   On the other hand, there is evidence that many people do not understand what is meant by "mediation", nor what the process entails, and

so they do not consider whether it might be appropriate for them, but seek other ways of resolving disputes. In order to promote the use of mediation, states may wish to improve information programmes in general and/or methods of providing information in individual cases. States may wish to make it compulsory for parties to meet with a mediator for the purpose of having the process of mediation and its benefits explained to them. Research indicates that such a meeting can be beneficial, and that parties appreciate the opportunity to resolve disputes amicably which such a meeting affords them. Nevertheless the essence of mediation itself rests in its voluntary character and on the fact that the parties themselves try to reach an agreement and if they refuse or feel unable to mediate, it is counter-productive to attempt to compel them.

29.   States, under this principle, are free to organise the provision of mediation as they wish, but as far as possible, states should ensure that there are mechanisms in place in order to maintain standards at an acceptable level.

30.   Within many states mediation is provided by private and public sectors working in collaboration or, conversely, in direct competition. At the present time, certain states are responsible for providing mediation services such as Andorra, Finland, Norway, Poland, Slovenia, Sweden and in some cases Germany. In some of these states, the municipal authorities are responsible. In all these states a mediation service is provided free of charge.

31.   In certain states such as Austria, France, Germany and the United Kingdom, mediation is primarily provided by institutions or individuals independent of the state. These mediators are not attached to courts, but may be attached to counselling, welfare or youth services. Any fees charged must be met by the parties themselves. The case of England and Wales is interesting as the Family Law Act 1996 makes provision for state funding for legal aid on a means-tested basis, and mediation agencies who wish to offer state-funded mediation must apply to be franchised for this purpose through the Legal Aid Board. In France legal aid is available to finance mediation requested by the court.

32.   Whatever the organisational arrangements, mediation should be available to all without any discrimination on the grounds of race, colour, language, religion or ethnicity. This may require mediation to be provided in a range of languages, or for interpreters to be available. Cultural differences must also be understood and respected.

33.   In addition, the Committee of Experts on Family Law (CJ-FA) considered questions relating to the selection, training and qualifications of mediators, believing that mediators should have previous qualifications and experience in relation to the matters to be dealt with as well as specific training in mediation. It was noted however, that it is desirable to allow a high degree of flexibility in relation to previous qualifications and experience, although most often mediators are drawn from the professions of social work, psychology and law.

34.   States should, wherever possible, ensure that there are appropriate procedures for the selection, training and qualifications of mediators, and for setting the standards to be achieved and maintained by mediators. Such procedures exist in some states. As there are two separate matters – selection, training and qualifications on the one hand, and the setting of standards on the other – not all states will have provisions for both.

35.   The characteristics of training will differ between states, although there is an increasing respect for training which includes the teaching of theoretical and specialist knowledge and also the opportunity to practice under expert supervision. In many states systems for the accreditation and professional registration of family mediators are being established. Experiments concerning education and training are being carried out in both the public and private sector in certain states.

36.   Although mediation is not yet regarded as a separate profession in all states, many states are developing guidelines for good practice, and establishing codes of conduct. It is probably premature to implement more formal requirements in this area until mediation is more widely practised at a European level. However, in the context of actions by states to ensure efficient and professional organisation for family mediation, there is nothing to prevent states if they so wish, from laying down provisions governing the activities and professional conduct of mediators.

Principle III: Process of mediation

37.   It is now widely agreed that mediation should be conducted according to certain principles which mark it out from other interventions or dispute-resolution mechanisms. This principle sets out these guidelines of practice in some detail.

38.   "Impartiality" of the mediator requires that the mediator does not take sides or favour the position of one party over the other. The views of each party should be respected, although the mediator has a duty to ensure that one party is not disadvantaged through fear of harm or threat of violence. The mediator should conduct the process in such a way as to redress, as far as possible, any imbalance in power between the parties, and should seek to prevent manipulative, threatening or intimidating behaviour by either of them. Unlike a lawyer, who acts for one of the parties and represents that party's point of view, the mediator is not acting for either party, nor should there be a previous or existing professional or personal relationship between the mediator and one of the parties.

39.   "Neutrality" of the mediator requires that the mediator does not impose settlements or guide the parties to reach particular solutions. It is up to the parties to reach their own agreed, joint decisions, and the mediator's role is to facilitate this process. Parties may make decisions which they consider to be appropriate to their own particular circumstances. This recognises the power of the parties to reach their own agreements about their own affairs in a way that suits them best. However, it is clear from paragraph 49 that when courts are asked to endorse or ratify such a private agreement then it will be

172

necessary that courts are satisfied that the settlements comply with current legislation and do not infringe either party's legitimate interests.

40.   Mediation should be conducted in private, and the discussions should be regarded as confidential. This means that the mediator should not disclose any information about, or obtained during the process of, mediation to anyone without either the express consent of each party or in cases allowed by national law. Whether a mediator has a right to refuse to give evidence in court is left to national law. The mediator should not be obliged to make official reports as to the content and discussions in mediation, although mediators may be expected to provide a report agreed by the parties to the judicial or other competent authority noting the agreements reached.

41.   It is usually expected that the parties should agree that the discussions and negotiations are not to be referred to in any subsequent legal proceedings. Such confidentiality is normally referred to as "privilege". The privilege belongs to the parties jointly, not to the mediator or the process. It can be waived by the parties and the mediator could be compelled to testify in legal proceedings. Mediators are likely to be bound by professional codes of conduct in relation to confidentiality but it is the parties who own privilege. This is a matter which states will wish to consider in the light of national law and standards of professional conduct.

42.   It is usually accepted that free and frank disclosure is necessary in mediation if obstacles to settlement are to be overcome. It is important, therefore, for the limits of confidentiality to be understood at the outset. At the beginning of mediation, parties should be informed that confidentiality cannot be absolute. Statements made during the course of mediation which indicate that a child has suffered or is at risk of suffering serious harm or abuse may be disclosed by the mediator and the parties may be encouraged to seek help from an appropriate agency or authority. In such circumstances, the child's best interests and welfare take priority over the considerations in respect of confidentiality. Member states may wish to specify other circumstances or cases in which confidentiality should be waived.

43.   During the process of separation and divorce, parties may benefit from the services of professionals other than mediators and lawyers. It is important, therefore, that the couples are made aware of other agencies who might offer them support, or particular types of help such as marital counselling. Bearing in mind the significant development and growth of alternative dispute-resolution mechanisms, the mediator should be aware of the options, and in appropriate cases, inform the parties about them.

44.   There appears to be a professional consensus that mediators should be sensitive to the issue of domestic violence. Mediators increasingly ensure that mechanisms are in place to ascertain the existence of an abusive relationship before agreeing to mediate. If one party is in fear of another party, bargaining positions will be unequal and the mediator may wish to terminate the mediation process. There is research evidence, however, which suggests that the fact that violence has been a feature of the relationship in the past should not automatically preclude the possibility that mediation is an

appropriate process. States will wish to consider this matter in the light of national law relating to domestic violence.

45.   Since most mediation is about making suitable and appropriate arrangements for children, mediators should have a special concern for the welfare and best interests of children whilst respecting their impartiality and neutrality and should remind parents of the need to inform and consult their children about what is happening, and that family disputes and prolonged conflict have a severe negative impact on children. In some states, mediators include children in the mediation process, usually at the end in order to let them hear about the arrangements which have been agreed between the parents. There are provisions in some states for children to attend mediation if this is thought to be in their interests. There is increasing emphasis on hearing the voice of the child in proceedings which affect him or her, and some mediation services provide children's counselling support, or contact centres where children can meet with their parents when access is difficult. States should be free to encourage the development of support services for children and young people whose parents are separating (see also paragraphs 55 and 59 below).

46.   During its deliberations, the Committee of Experts on Family Law (CJ-FA) considered the limitations of the mediator's role, particularly with regard to the giving of legal information and legal advice. It is agreed that a distinction should be made between advice and information, and that it is appropriate for mediators to provide legal information if this is requested or considered to be appropriate during the mediation process. Information-giving involves maintaining a relationship of impartiality with the parties. Information is given as a resource without any attempt to recommend how it should be acted upon. For example, it may be helpful for parties to know what legal steps might be taken to resolve disputes if agreements cannot be reached in mediation; or what factors a judge might take into consideration when making a decision about custody, access or child maintenance.

47.   On the other hand, advice-giving is in contradiction with one of the principles of mediation, namely impartiality. Advice-giving includes the evaluation of particular circumstances and the recommendation of a specific course of action. Lawyers give both legal information and legal advice to their clients but mediators would be compromising their neutrality and impartiality if they were to give legal advice. Lawyers and mediators have complementary roles, and mediators will suggest, if necessary, that parties should seek legal advice from their lawyers, who are trained to recommend actions which are in each party's best interests. In states where mediation is well developed, mediators usually advise parties to seek independent legal advice before reaching any legally binding agreement.

48.   There is no requirement in the recommendation in relation to the duration of mediation. It will vary depending on the number and nature of issues in dispute and the complexity involved. Nevertheless, mediation is expected to be a relatively brief intervention, and not an opportunity for ongoing or longer-term professional support. Usually, the mediators and the parties agree on the matters to be discussed in mediation, and the number of

mediation meetings which might take place. It is a matter for individual states to decide whether they wish to regulate the length of the mediation process, or to ensure that mediation cannot be used by one party purely as a means of delaying the divorce process.

Principle IV: The status of mediated agreements

49.	In most states, the agreements reached in mediation are recorded and copies given to the parties who might then take them to their lawyers. Such agreements are not normally legally binding, although there is considerable variation between states on this matter at the present time. Even where the agreements are legally binding however, as in Germany and Norway for example, they are not usually enforceable unless and until they have been endorsed by the appropriate judicial or other competent authority. One of the methods of complying with these principles would be for the judicial or other competent authority to incorporate the results of mediation into its own decision. In endorsing or ratifying agreements, a judicial or other competent authority must check that the settlements comply with current legislation and do not infringe on either party's legitimate interests, and in particular that the best interests of children are protected.

50.	Since research in the United Kingdom and other countries has shown that some people who use mediation are disappointed when their agreements do not carry the same weight or authority as court-imposed solutions, it is recommended that states should facilitate the possibility of approval by a judicial or other competent authority within the framework of their own family legislation. In this regard, it should be possible for the mediator to assist parties to draw up a statement of agreements in a manner that renders it acceptable by the judicial or other competent authority as a relevant "legal" document for the purposes of ratification and approval.

51.	If parties do not choose to ask a judicial or other competent authority to endorse their agreement, the agreement will have the same legal status as any other private law contract and will last only as long as the parties apply it. On the other hand, where the agreement is approved by a judicial or other competent authority at the request of parties, one party can bring proceedings before this authority if the other party fails to comply with it.

52.	In recommending that states facilitate the approval of mediated agreements by the relevant authority and provide mechanisms for the enforcement of such agreements, it was noted that the establishment of such mechanisms could contribute significantly to the credibility of, and respect for, mediation.

53.	Any mechanism for securing approval by the judicial or other competent authority should not lead to delay or excessive costs.

Principle V: Relationships between mediation and the proceedings before the judicial or other competent authority

175

54.   Other competent authorities have been included in the recommendation in addition to the judicial authorities as the powers which belong to courts are also, in some states, exercised by administrative authorities for certain types of family proceedings.

55.   As regards the right of access to the courts, it is possible for the parties to mediation to waive the exercise of this right provided that such a waiver is unequivocal and voluntary (see paragraph 1 of Article 6 of the European Convention on Human Rights and the case law on this article).

56.   This principle reaffirms the belief that mediation should be an entirely autonomous process. As such, mediation can take place before, during or after legal proceedings, although it is commonly accepted that mediation is more effective if it can take place before, or early in legal proceedings. Mediating disputes is generally more difficult if the conflict has escalated and the disputes are of long duration. Before legal proceedings are commenced, parties are less likely to have adopted fixed positions on disputes from which it is hard for them to shift or to make compromises, and they may be more amenable to negotiating agreements.

57.   When mediation takes place during legal proceedings, those legal proceedings should be interrupted, constituting a temporary adjournment or suspension of the process. As mediation is a voluntary process, each party should normally give agreement for legal proceedings to be suspended. This avoids one party using mediation as a way of causing delays in legal proceedings. Unnecessary delays in the decision-making process are considered to be harmful, particularly for children. Time delays may also increase the financial costs to the parties and to the state.

58.   When proceedings are suspended for the purpose of enabling parties to seek mediation, however, the judicial or other competent authority retains the power at all times to make urgent decisions in order to protect the parties, their children, or their property.

59.   When proceedings are interrupted, then mechanisms should exist to inform the judicial or other competent authority when mediation is complete, and for the mediator to report on the outcomes and agreements reached, and for this authority to review whether these agreements are protecting the best interests of children.

60.   Judges and the courts need to retain their ultimate authority in the legal process, and may be required to consider the facts, make decisions and impose a solution which protects and upholds individual human rights, the best interests of children, and ensures access to justice.

61.   After proceedings have been completed, whether agreements have been mediated, or decisions imposed by the judicial or other competent authority, new disputes may arise, previous disputes may re-emerge, or one or all parties may seek to change existing arrangements due to changed circumstances. In these cases, it may be appropriate to return to mediation, or go to mediation for the first time, in order to attempt

to reach a settlement without recourse to instituting further legal proceedings. At all times, mediation should be entered into voluntarily.

62.   Nothing in this principle implies that the court has the power to appoint a mediator.

Principle VI: Promotion of, and access to, mediation

63.   In establishing this principle it was acknowledged that mediation has not been well understood or well used in most states. Surveys have shown that, when asked, people think that resolving disputes amicably is preferable to litigation, but few have heard of mediation services, or mediators.

64.   In order to improve knowledge and understanding about mediation, states should promote mechanisms for informing the public through information programmes, written materials, and the media. It is particularly important to ensure that lawyers and the judicial or other competent authorities understand the mediation process and can provide accurate information to parties who may wish to use it.

65.   While there is some information available in most states about mediation services, only in Andorra and Norway have there been national campaigns to provide information. In England and Wales, the Family Law Act 1996 requires attendance by the party wishing to initiate divorce proceedings, at an information meeting during which verbal, written and other information will be provided on a number of matters, including mediation. It will also be possible, if a party is seeking legal aid for legal representation, to require attendance at a meeting with a mediator in order that the suitability of the case for mediation can be considered and the mediation process and potential benefits explained. Attendance at such meetings may be compulsory, and states are free to consider the advantages of such a procedure.

66.   It is a fundamental principle that if mediation is introduced as an alternative dispute-resolution process, it should be available to all who might wish to use it. Access to mediation could be promoted by states for example, by providing some financial support for mediation services directly, or by providing legal aid to parties on the same basis as for legal proceedings.

Principle VII: Other means of resolving disputes

67.   The recommendation clearly recognises that mediation is not the only process available for settling disputes in an amicable, consensual way. Others include:

a.   conciliation, or conciliation counselling, which are frequently used as alternative terms for mediation. It describes a process of orderly discussion under the guidance of a neutral third party, known as a conciliator.

b.   family counselling, although more commonly describing a process in which a neutral third party helps parties to understand and work through

177

difficulties with a view to saving or restoring a relationship, can assist parties to make agreements about a future life apart.

68.   As all such means of resolving disputes without recourse to the courts and litigation are to be encouraged, the recommendation indicates that states may examine the desirability of applying the principles of mediation, as laid out in this recommendation, to these other processes. However, no two processes of dispute resolution should be ongoing simultaneously, since this may cause interference or confusion for the parties, and thus undermine the benefits of the different processes.

Principle VIII: International matters

69.   This principle recognises the increasing number of family disputes, particularly concerning custody and access, in which there is an international element. It recognises also that in these cases international mediation should be considered as an appropriate process.

70.   During the discussions, the following situations were considered:

a.   the fixing of conditions for access;

b.   access to a child who has been returned after an improper removal;

c.   the cases where there has been a refusal to return the child by a court decision;

d.   the cases where the child is opposed to access or custody.

71.   International mediation should be considered as an appropriate process in order to help parents to organise or re-organise custody and/or access, or to resolve disputes arising after decisions have been made in cases where parents are resident in different states. Such disputes are frequently the most difficult to manage because of the transfrontier nature, and the involvement of more than one judicial or other competent authority.

72.   Family mediation could be a useful process in order to fix the conditions for access, in particular safeguards and guarantees that in cases of transfrontier access the child is returned at the end of the access period, before any decision has been reached when parents are living or plan to live in different states.

73.   Mediation could also be useful in the following situations:

a.   cases where the recognition or enforcement of the decision relating to custody is refused by the court of the state addressed (this is the state to which the child has been removed) on the basis of a ground of refusal established in an international instrument (for instance, grounds of refusal established in Article 10 of the European Convention on Recognition and Enforcement of Decisions concerning Custody of Children and on Restoration of Custody of Children of 1980), and the applicant parent requested the

178

institution of fresh proceedings concerning the substance of the case (Article 5, paragraph 4 of the Custody Convention);

b.   cases when the applicant (custodian parent) accepts the refusal by the court of the state addressed to recognise and enforce the decision relating to custody but requests the central authority of that state to apply to the court for granting access (Article 11, paragraph 3 of the Custody Convention).

74.   All the principles of mediation in this recommendation apply to international mediation. In addition there are some specific considerations in international cases:

a.   there may be good reasons why the parties may wish to mediate in a particular state (country/culture of origin, for example) and wherever possible, parties should be free to choose where mediation takes place. States should look at the issues and work together co-operatively to ensure that the best possible opportunities for mediation exist for parties experiencing transfrontier disputes. It may be that a third state might provide a more neutral territory for mediation when parties are resident in different states.

b.   the need for specific additional training for international mediators in order to take account of a number of specific factors. International mediators will have to take account of the family law systems pertaining to the states where parents are or will be habitually resident and the essential principles of international instruments relating to custody, access and child abduction. In addition consideration will have to be given to the particular difficulties parents will encounter when they are making arrangements for access across national boundaries and geographical distances and the fears of custodial parents in respect of child abduction, which may be heightened as a result of the non-custodial parent living in another state and jurisdiction. Any special risks and consequences of child abduction will also have to be considered. International mediators will also have to take account of different cultural expectations in the countries in which the parties are going to be resident which may impact on how the parties perceive their responsibilities as parents, and how they may respond to changing circumstances. Account will also have to be taken of the cultural influences of extended family members, in particular grandparents, in respect of arrangements for access and the upbringing of a child. International mediators will need to work flexibly (using a variety of models, for example shuttle mediation, video conferencing and so on) in order to mediate across distances and will need the knowledge of foreign languages or the competency and training in the appropriate use of interpreters and other experts as deemed necessary in any specific case.

75.   International mediation may require different forms of mediation, such as shuttle mediation for example. Shuttle mediation refers to the way the mediator may act as a go-between, shuttling between the two parties who remain physically apart. The mediator may pass messages between them, or actively negotiate on behalf of the parties. It is a common method in international mediation. There are disadvantages, however, particularly if the mediator does all the negotiating, and is at risk of compromising neutrality and impartiality.

76.   In some cases it may be necessary to conduct a mediation meeting by tele-conference, or to involve more than one mediator. Co-mediation may offer distinct advantages where there is particularly intense conflict, or difficult circumstances, as are frequently found in international disputes.

77.   In the case of transfrontier access, international mediation has advantages over other procedures:

a.   it gives the responsibility of making arrangements about custody and access to the parents themselves;

b.   it facilitates the work of the judge in what can be very difficult cases;

c.   it can reduce the costs of litigation.

78.   In cases of wrongful removal or retention of a child, mediation may not be advisable during pending return proceedings. There is an obligation based on international instruments to return the child immediately and therefore there must not be any delay. In such proceedings, however, mediation could be used for dilatory tactics. Furthermore in cases of wrongful removal or retention, states which have made use of the possibility given by Principle VI.b of the recommendation should normally not require the parent, whose right has been infringed, to meet a mediator before deciding on the return of the child. Moreover, mediation may not be appropriate because the wrongful removal or retention of a child adversely affects the equality of the parties' bargaining positions. After the end of the return proceedings mediation could be useful in re-establishing negotiations with a view to finding solutions in order to continue access in the best interests of the child.

79.   International mediation should be encouraged, therefore, but should not be mandatory. If parents are to be encouraged to mediate transfrontier disputes, there is a need to increase the information available for parents, and encourage co-operation between mediators in different states.

---

1. Conciliation counselling is mediation which includes some counselling.